the ABC's of BUREAUCRACY

the ABC's of BUREAUCRACY

Robert B. Jansen

Nelson Hall/Chicago

Library of Congress Cataloging in Publication Data

Jansen, Robert B., 1922-
   The ABC's of bureaucracy.

   Includes index.
   1. Bureaucracy.   I. Title.
JF1501.J35   350'.001   78-1840
ISBN 0-88229-331-1

Manufactured in the United States of America

10   9   8   7   6   5   4   3   2   1

Contents

Chapter 1

Introduction

This primer on bureaucracy comes to you from real life in the bureaucratic morass. Some of the creatures found in this habitat may look familiar. Their resemblance to humans of your acquaintance is intentional.

The counsel here unfolded is for those who aspire to careers in government. It is drawn from the experiences of the authoritative elite in city halls, statehouses, and the nation's capital, where the bureaucratic mentality has evolved to its highest form.

Bureaucracy is a part of modern life. Its caress has been laid upon commerce without favoritism or exception. Every corner of society is under its shelter. Though not confined to government, it has reached fullest development as an integral element of the governing process. Knowledge of its many facets is essential to success in the regulatory arena. Those who would not stoop to use it nor rise to deal with it would undoubtedly be more comfortable in some place where it does not exist, if there is such a place.

In the bureaucratic environment an incompetent can find sanctuary and a good worker can meet frustrating challenge that demands all his strength. The test is to get something done without getting lost in the labyrinth. The system itself is the adversary. Nobody defeats it. But the accomplished bureaucrat learns to orchestrate its movements, to play its instruments, and to suffer its discordant strains.

In this environment, some of the traditional concepts of organization and management tend to lose their meaning and effect. Assimilation of institutional principles is most important. As a matter of fact, a special theory of bureaucratic accommodation can be advanced which holds that *the rate of hierarchical ascent is in direct proportion to capacity for conformance.*

The aspirant who can suppress his individuality and embrace institutional norms lays a sound base for advancement. If he has the further ability to sense the moods and prejudices and desires of his superiors and to adjust readily to accommodate their needs, he can stay aboard his bureaucratic balloon for the ride to the top. This loyal chameleon will be generously rated by those in the upper layers. The mantle of compliance that he wears may obscure inconsequential characteristics such as laziness, moral deficiency, or ignorance. But few in the executive chambers will probe his privacy as long as he wears the official colors.

The placement of substantial numbers of such people in the strata of the hierarchy does not cause significant damage. That is the beauty of it. A well-constituted bureaucracy almost runs by itself. In fact, strong personalities might weaken it. Only an overwhelming invasion of nonconformists could seriously threaten its existence. And this is not very likely to happen. Nonconformists are seldom attracted to the maze.

There is some fear that bureaucracy will eventually smother civilization. Such concern reflects lack of insight into the physiology of the bureau organism. It is largely an uncoordinated being, with loose tendons and viscous body fluids. Certainly it is massive, and therefore terrifying to some who stand in its shadow, but its brain cells are not unified enough to focus on malice. Like some lower forms of animal, it may contract into its shell when threatened with attack. Basically sedentary, its movements are seldom vigorous, although an overnourished tentacle may lash out from time to time. An enormous intake fuels its rumbling bowels and stimulates its growth. But it is not a people-eater. On the contrary, people-parasites are embedded in its skin and it does not even scratch them.

Many voices have been raised in condemnation of bureaucracy for being slow in its responses and resistant to evolution. The criticism is misguided. These attributes which are so generally assailed should instead be showered with acclaim. By standing in the way of reformers and revolutionaries and tyrants, the bureaucratic monster defends the people's rights and way of life. It may not do so knowingly, but just by being there blocking the road it achieves its vital purpose.

Continuity and stability of governments and of civilizations depend to a large extent upon the bureaucracies which support them. Longevity varies with the strength of bureaucratic anchorage. To do lasting good, a government must stay in power for more than a little while. It cannot do this through oratory alone. The mount on which it rides must be sturdy. Ideally it would be indestructible. A well-muscled bureaucracy meets these requirements.

Leaders themselves are expendable. Tradition alone dictates that there be somebody at the top of the pyramid, but who it is may not matter as much as how he adjusts to the system. A chief executive can have little lasting effect without the bureaucratic carrier, upon which he and his predecessor and his successor rely each in his time.

Some leaders, particularly those thrust into power in a hurry, mistakenly assume that they themselves are the government. They may be frustrated by the revelation that the bureaucracy is really running things. Feeling obligated to make changes in the name of progress, they will find that ordering it does not make it so.

A chief who expects so much and gets so little in bureaucratic response may feel that this brands him as a failure. Subscribing to the common notion that governmental accomplishment stems from and is measured by executive edict and legislative outpouring, he understandably will have great difficulty in adjusting when the bureaus slam on the brakes. The massive organization, which he thought belonged to him, looms as an immovable barrier thwarting all his ambitions.

The wise leader, after making a traumatic adjustment, may see one of the most important truths: *Bureaucracy performs an indispensable function of stabilizing and preserving a government and the civilization which it serves.* It is the essential bulwark against the willful and the overzealous and the evil who would aspire to lead. Without it, the people would not know from day to day what their government was going to do to them next.

Undoubtedly some citizens do not see bureaucracy in this favorable light. They see it attacked regularly by those who yearn for change, and they share the widespread resentment aimed at the multitude of embedded civil servants who will not let changes happen. Citizens take it for granted that elected officials are suspect, but theoretically at least they can be removed when they become obviously villainous. When the ballot winds blow, however, politicians may become contortionists while career bureaucrats remain unmoved and even unreachable.

Bureaulings themselves, for the most part, are not aware of the significance of their individual and institutional contributions to the well-being of the nation. Confined to their cells in the maze they tend to see only to the next turn in the corridor. If asked why they are there, they may answer that they have nowhere else to go. While this may be true, it is not entirely relevant. Although their individual motivations may be unworthy of commendation, collectively they are the cement which holds the country together.

There is a little bit of bureaucracy in nearly any organization. It can be found in factories, schools, and fraternal lodges. Hardly any of these, however, can match the organisms that thrive in government. While bureaucracy exists everywhere, it permeates the pores of government most completely.

Uninformed critics have likened government to a lethargic creature moving in imponderable ways. This would suggest a giant snail or slug devouring tremendous volumes of memoranda and standard forms and depositing a slimy excrement which offers uncertain footing for those who would try to follow. This is far from the truth. There is really nothing in government so imponderable that it cannot be explained. In fact, there are specialists who do nothing but explain how it works.

The bureaucracy is impenetrable due to the armor plate riveted over it by the legislative protectors. Although many of its haters would like to skin it and peck away at its flesh, it is seldom actually menaced. When harassment brings it even the slightest uneasiness, it withdraws into the recesses until the abuse subsides.

With much of society diffusing its energies on various forms of idealistic experiment, the bureau is by contrast a bulwark against disruptive action. If the merits of stalemate are recognized, the benevolent inertia of the bureaucratic discipline can be appreciated. Activists have foundered on this rock without ever seeing it. Immobility is assured by traditions which tend to be preserved beyond the memory of their origin. As long as the members of the institution are comfortable with them they will endure and take precedence over the demands of the external world.

In contrast to the kaleidoscopic universe of the politician, bureaudom is a mosaic of undramatic pattern. Its inlaid functional fragments provide essential stability. There is seldom anything haphazard about the organizational structure of a bureaucracy. Each piece interlocks with another to assure rigidity.

Although there is always an impressive flow of new rules disgorging from the legislative and administrative machinery, many of the additive requirements are froth wafted over a stationary base. Procedures are piled upon procedures, thus lengthening the process. But this is not change in a real sense. No matter how many gears and wheels are attached, the bureaucratic train tends to stay on the same track.

Of course, new programs are added from time to time, and are laid down alongside the old. There is seldom resistance to this kind of change within the system. Multiplication of activities stimulates expansion of the bureau and its attendant strengthening of security and advancement opportunity. Overseers need not fear the increased workload since accountability for everything is widely shared. However, expansion is sometimes accompanied by innovation. This can be troublesome. To avoid disruption of flow in the channels, any injection of ideas must be filtered to remove contamination. The atmosphere of the bureau must be kept sanitary and cleansed of adulterating elements.

There are many kinds of bureaucracies and bureaucrats. They cannot be described simply, although many of them have recognizable similarities. They have been maligned and sometimes praised. A fair evaluator would have to concede that they do have their place. Although many of them function primarily as retardants, there have been a few who have been instruments of change. The newer regulatory agencies deserve a large share of the credit for this. Some critics say that these are not true bureaucracies, because they seek action rather than avoid it. In some ways, though, these agencies can be just as obstructive as those who openly adhere to this tradition. While the new regulators do advocate reform and therefore rate as activists, they may at the same time do their level best to see that actions sought by others are impeded. This is in the noblest of bureaucratic traditions.

What is a bureaucrat? In the governmental setting he or she may be a postal clerk or a cabinet officer, or anything in between. Classifications based on modus operandi or personal inclination may range from Cautious Avoider (found in large numbers in the Federal Power Commission) to Wild-Eyed Intervener (reportedly populous in the Environmental Protection Agency). The many who reside and take their sustenance in the labyrinth are not all commonly known as bureaucrats. Some are referred to simply as civil servants or public employees. By the broadest definition they are all bureaucrats. No matter what they are called, they are the resident beneficiaries of the system. People of quite modest capabilities have been known to thrive in this environment.

Bureaucrats have been described as people somehow different from ordinary human beings, with different motivations and different attitudes. The truth is that their mainsprings are not wound any more tightly or loosely than the mechanisms of average men and women on the street. They take care of themselves because others are unlikely to do it for them. This does not set them apart from the masses.

The bureaucratic habitat is sometimes likened to a primitive jungle where the animals do what comes naturally. This comparison has only limited validity. Bureaucrats are usually not nearly as fierce as the beasts of the jungle. They may stand up and fight when their nests are invaded, but only a few are predatory. They feel comfortable in their tribal compounds and will not venture out to disturb others without considerable cause. While they may exhibit some of the instincts of the herd, they are not inclined to stampede. In fact, some of them are reluctant to move at all.

This is not to say that conflict is uncommon in the bureaucracy. Much of the strife that does exist stems from the strong desire of the masses to preserve their environment. Any suggestion of change can be disquieting. Nothing upsets the bureau more than uncertainty. This is when bureaucratic executives rise to the challenge. To prove themselves as true leaders they must resist change in the conditions in the labyrinth.

Any healthy bureaucracy will tend to enlarge as it takes nourishment. This helps its members to gain in status. To assure that more share in the prestige of elevation, the pyramid can be built higher with more intermediate levels as resting points. Bureaucratic position is nearly always enhanced by enlargement of agencies, broadening of their functions, and the swelling of their populations. This is not always easily done. Bureaucrats have to work hard to expand their spheres. Aggressive salesmanship is needed to inflate budgets to the necessary levels and to persuade constituencies of the benefits.

With the multiplication of governmental units at all levels and the mushrooming of dependent constituencies, there is actually no way for government to be quick. Huddling and handholding and group massage are indispensable if the interests of a multitude of demanders are to be treated. In fact, the governments in all echelons are locking arms and moving in cadence. If there is a trend in government, this is it. The apparent cooperation is less voluntary than of necessity. The problems have grown to such an extent that more bureaucrats are needed to share the responsibility. None of this need be alarming. On the contrary, comfort can be found in the growth and compounding of bureaucratic institutions. The broader the base, the stronger the structure.

The need for expansion is easily explained. Most assignments in the bureau are continuing activities which presumably had a justified beginning but do not have any foreseeable ending. Yet much rhetoric is given to the need to bring a job to completion. To mount a credible assault upon this goal, reinforcements must be called up and effort must be doubled. Since each member is already producing to a preset limit, more people are required to be added to the staff to intensify the effort. As more participants crowd in, the number of perceptions of what needs to be done is multiplied. The job is thus enlarged and its completion may become even more distant.

The units of a bureau normally will grow in proportion to the expansion of the parent organization, and the parts may tend to take on the characteristics of the whole. Expanding staff units become increasingly complex. The objectives of the staff may deviate from those of the bureau in which it resides. To further its own purposes, it may serve its masters less than it serves itself. As its war with the line units in the bureau intensifies, the staff may control the flow of information to the bureau's leaders so that decisions will be made in its favor, if any decisions are made. A staff hierarchy that rates as truly bureaucratic will lead the chief executive to embrace staff ideas and to believe that they are his own. One of those ideas that is essential is that the staff must exercise authority no matter what the textbooks say. A chief executive properly indoctrinated will be easily persuaded that the final word on important activities must come from his immediate staff.

Agencies bursting at the seams and strained by internal competitions are not noted for clear policies. Such bureaucracies are not the sole contributors to the confusion which befogs the land, but as generators of vapor they are practically without parallel. In most cases they have not set out to confuse. This contrasts bureaucrats with some officials with a more political orientation.

Bureaucratic agencies normally move in straight lines and at predictable speeds, which are usually slow. This is because of the involvement of so many in the voluminous procedural details that must be developed to support any movement. The methodical approach of the agency toward any contemplated action has merits which deserve mention. It exposes ill-conceived ideas to lengthy scrutiny. They may still get adopted if advocates are insistent enough, but in the meantime nothing happens to disrupt the tranquility of the established order.

Government must play its role in the making of decisions no matter how long it takes. Many agencies want to be involved but not very many really want to make decisions. This assures that each project will be thoroughly examined before the green light is flashed. The rising cost of governmental decisions has been widely and fully discussed. Some critics raise questions about the difficulty of pinpointing responsibility for the actions which issue from the labyrinth. As long as nobody has the answer, the system is assured of a long life.

Once its manual has been written and everybody has memorized the rules, the work of a bureau is comparatively easy. If it keeps the same number of people it can afford plenty of wasted motion. The routinized tasks, once the organization has matured, will hardly keep the staff busy. This allows time for satisfying the individual needs of the inhabitants, as well as poking around in the territory of other agencies. Efficiency experts would argue that an agency which can function with fewer employees should do so. But very few bureaucratic leaders will volunteer a reduction of their staffs to a level that is just enough. An agency which has reached a stable plateau must keep up the same appearances year after year so that nobody will doubt its stability or its permanency. Even if its so-called workload sputters and spurts, the bureau must make it look as if it is smoothly flowing in high volume. Every dollar of the budget must be spent to maintain this proud image. Maintenance will be made easier if somehow the bureau can invent or appropriate additional responsibilities. Although the manual makes the bureau relatively inflexible in its procedures, the objectives of the agency can be varied enough to cope with the changing threats to its survival. As long as the bureau is able to shift its course, nobody need worry much about its demise once it has passed its early adolescence.

The longevity of a bureau, however, is not fully

guaranteed. Even though nearly all bureaus appear to be permanent fixtures, the obstacles which an agency faces may be considerable. Fortunately it usually has more than enough resources to cope with them. A bureau with expansionist tendencies does stimulate competition by other bureaucracies, especially those who may be threatened by encroachment. Even without competition, a bureau will have to smear ample cosmetics on its image to cover its tendency to grow stagnant as it ages. As the population of the bureau increases, the mean level of competence will drop and more and more money may be required just to maintain a constant level of output, let alone to support rates of expansion. If it satisfies its basic constituency and is unable to muster additional support for its services, opportunities for the bureau's inhabitants will decline and talent will drain or tend to lose luster. The aggressors who remain are likely to turn away from the repetitive functions which gave the bureau its reason for existence. They may find satisfaction then in bureaucratic infighting. This will keep them lean and mean and ready for challenges if such should develop.

An agency which has been around for a while usually operates with its engines throttled, consuming plenty of fuel but still having some capacity for greater output if the need arises. This reserve capability, made possible by a surplus of people, is helpful to a bureau in several ways. With everybody carrying only part of a load, nobody gets strained or disturbed—unless asked to carry a full load. The storehouse of energy in the bureau is a source of comfort throughout the labyrinth because it represents a form of insulation against unpleasant surprises. With so many people around working at less than their maximum rate, the system has flexibility in abundance. Adjustments to workload fluctuations are easy as long as a real emergency is not declared. The spare time available after two or three hours a day of routine agency business can be used to pursue the individual interests of the bureau's inhabitants, allowing them satisfactions which could never be realized in an organization working at full blast.

In theory, at least, an organization moving in low gear has an enormous potential for acceleration when adequate incentives are provided. In the meantime, while such challenge is awaited, the cost of maintaining the standby capability may be considerable. Those who would criticize do not see the tremendous storehouse of promise in an idling bureaucracy waiting to be aroused. The things that the bureaulings do in the meantime to keep themselves occupied may not be seen as contributory to the interests of the citizenry at large. Yet the pressures to reduce the populations of bureaucracies are seldom intense. Bureaucrats are evidently not held in as much disfavor as some dissident taxpayers would like to believe. Those who contemplate inquiry into bureaucratic inefficiencies can usually be isolated and persuaded to be more reasonable. Would-be investigators may be amenable to reciprocity when confronted with the array of favors that the bureaucracy can dispense.

No bureaucracy can endure long, however, without constituencies which can provide its sustenance. The advantages that it offers must be evident to those who have the power to make it or break it. Constituencies who can profit disproportionately from its existence will tend to lend it enough support to outweigh the opposition of those who may object to its high cost. One of the biggest advantages that nearly any bureaucracy has is the large body of the citizenry which is not interested enough to give it attention. By concentrating on its beneficiaries, and even organizing and orchestrating their support, an agency can set itself on a track from which it will not be easily derailed. An alliance forged between dispensers and receivers, as in a welfare agency, is not likely to be broken. The arrangement will be even more secure if those from whom the necessary funds are taken are kept ignorant of the cost. With the complexity of the taxing systems, this has not been difficult.

Much has been said about bureaucratic momentum, but its nature has been badly misunderstood. In fact, the bureaucracy sometimes has moved like an unstoppable locomotive only because it was fueled by the exaggerated commitments of elected officials. Laws have been passed which opened money faucets that cannot be turned off. Bureaucrats, of course, are among the beneficiaries of this largess so they cannot be expected to crank the faucets down very hard. There are bureaucracies that have nothing to do but take money away from one group and give it to another. The benevolence of this is not showered only upon the direct recipients. It is also very worthwhile for those who handle the money as it passes from one hand to the other. The people employed by the welfare agencies can attest to this.

Even though bureaucracy is frowned upon in some corners of society, its image with most of the people is attractive enough to assure its survival and expansion. If this were not true, the rapid multiplication of government bureaus would not be sustainable. A brief look at the statistics of bureaucratic expansion gives assurance that the common man likes plenty of government. In 1930 expenditures of all echelons of government in the United States amounted to approximately 10 percent of the personal income of its citizens. Ten years later this had doubled to 20 percent, and by 1975 it had reached about 40 percent. Some of the credit for the establishment of this new record was deserved by legislators throughout the land who were sensitive to the financial needs of the continuously expanding government agencies.

Evidently many Americans are appreciative of the increasing control that their government has exercised over their daily lives, protecting them from complexities and showering at least some of them with subsidy. By reading the printed instructions and filling in the blanks on the government's forms as instructed, a citizen can be comfortably insulated from the necessity to think for himself. While politicians in general have dropped a few notches on the scale of public confidence since the Watergate episode, the people are not turning their backs on profligate government. They still expect that sometime, somehow, the government will do something right.

At this point, I must declare where I stand on the bureaucracy. The reader deserves to know whence the information on these pages flows. It comes from my real experience in city, state, and federal agencies in the United States, from the lowest entry level to high civil service stratum.

My view is admittedly ambivalent. I have seen the bureaucracy at its worst and at its best. Perhaps this book will not show it in its most favorable light. Therefore, before we plunge on, let us strike some balance by examining an example of American government operating in a way that it can when it feels the incentive. The case in point was the investigation of the failure of the Teton Dam in Idaho on June 5, 1976, with tragic loss of life and hundreds of millions of dollars in property damage. This was the first failure of a major structure in the illustrious seventy-four-year history of the Bureau of Reclamation. Its parent agency, the U. S. Department of the Interior, wanted sincerely to find out what had caused the disaster. So did the state of Idaho. With this imperative purpose, the governor of that state and the Secretary of the Interior jointly sponsored an independent panel to review the failure and charged it with finding the cause and reporting thereon within six months. The task of the panel was difficult.

I know, because I was its executive director. What is pertinent here, though, is how the federal and state governments shouldered their responsibilities. In the first place, they allowed the panel to be truly independent even though the potential consequences of its findings were worrisome. The Secretary of the Interior put out the word that administrative obstacles were to be cleared away so that the investigation could be expedited. He saw that his best people were assigned to assure this. Talented and conscientious government workers from Portland, Boise, Idaho Falls, Denver, Albuquerque, and Washington, D.C., provided needed services in support of the investigating consultants. To meet the deadline, these people drawn from many places worked twelve-hour days and seven-day weeks. None of them complained. With hardly an exception, the quality of their work was outstanding. Yet, by the broadest definition, these people were bureaucrats.

A parallel example just as revealing is the California Water Project, a $3 billion undertaking unprecedented in any state of the Union. The government of the state of California committed itself fully to this venture and got it done within budget and on schedule. Its workers responded with competence and enthusiasm. They too could be defined as bureaucrats. I was with them, and can affirm that they were good people.

As the reader contrasts these experiences with the many less shining examples which follow in the book, he may well wonder about the bureaucratic highs and lows that they represent. The answer lies in the degree of dedication of the hierarchy. If the leaders really want it done, it will get done. If they are halfhearted, their followers will respond in kind. The best bureaucrats will do the job, no matter how many rules or how many lesser bureaucrats stand in the way. Their achievement is all the more commendable because nothing is easy for achievers in the labyrinth.

If bureaucracy is ever going to be improved, the impetus must start with the chief executive. On the federal scene currently, President Jimmy Carter is determined to cut red tape. He remembers that as Governor of Georgia his views on proposed federal laws and regulations were sometimes solicited and then disregarded. His office is pledged to involve state and local people in the writing of regulations. His director of the Office of Management and Budget said, "We've got to return to productivity instead of spending so much time on government paperwork." The OMB has strived to reduce the number of its forms. Interior Secretary Cecil Andrus has called for clear wording and reduced reporting in regulations written by his agency. OSHA Director Eula Bingham wants to end nit-picking. She freed 3.4 million small firms from reporting rules and cut paperwork in half for 1.5 million others, saving about $100 million yearly.

Moving ahead to take a closer look into the bureau's recesses, there should be no doubt that this is a nonfiction book. Although some parts are written with possibly detectable humor, the messages are serious. The examples that I offer are real, but no more so probably than those that come to mind from the reader's own experience. He will have seen both the good ones and the bad ones, and will know that there are not many flawless stereotypes.

Nobody who has witnessed the bureaucracy at close range is likely to volunteer seriously to be its defender or apologist. Any conscientious observer must concede its general creakiness and its retarding effect on many government actions. To give the monster its due, though, there must be some recognition of its value as a damper on the big drafts in the other government estates. Its laborious waddling provides more time for consideration of, and adjustment to, any program that may be proposed or imposed. Lubricating its joints might improve its efficiency, but thereby would reduce its usefulness as a drag.

Any citizen who has been paying attention to his government will have suggestions for improvements. There is a popular idea, for instance, that subtracting large numbers of bureaucrats from the public payroll would save great bundles of money, thus easing the burdens of taxpayers. Bureaucrats are indeed expensive, especially when you count the fringe benefits. However, in the American economic system, no matter what you do with these people, they still have to be fed, clothed, and housed. And if they don't have spending money they can't make their fair-share contribution to stimulation of the economy. Since nonbureaucrats must support them in any case, the real question which should be considered is whether bureaucrats do more bad than good.

In an imaginary world without governmental bureaucracy, all would not necessarily be utopian. For one thing, wayward politicians could then impose their wishes on the people immediately without filtration. Also, the lineup of former bureaucrats at the welfare offices would be so overwhelming that handouts to the usual recipients would be long delayed. In fact, it would hardly be worth their effort since those offices would be unmanned, as would practically all civilian government facilities except those occupied by elected officials.

In that suddenly chaotic world, nonbureaucrats would be surrounded and almost outnumbered by millions of unemployed civil servants. Among the milling ranks would be the tax collectors and custodians of the printing presses at the mint. With these facilities idle, the government would be deprived of easy money, and would have to dip directly into the pockets of the citizenry to sustain itself. The whole thing is completely unthinkable.

A sincere conclusion which must be drawn from such conjectural meandering is that a bureaucracy of some kind is essential to provide basic functions and to assure checks and balances. I honestly believe that the bureaucracy—efficient or not—is valuable to damp the influence of politics. The nation is more than two hundred years old, and our elected representatives have been making laws during all that time. There are too many laws. But one-way government traffic locks them into our lives. The bureaucrats soften their impact.

Bureaucratic systems in government are of course not uniquely American. They have long histories in Europe and in Asia. Somehow most of those countries have survived. Unpersuaded by their obvious durability you may still ask why government bureaucracies can't be more efficient. Some analysts would cite the lack of profit motive. Others would say that public employment attracts mediocre performers. There may be a little bit of merit in each of these arguments. But the fact remains that a few nonprofit agencies are productive. How do they do it? One essential is a well-defined mission whose results will be visible. An agency so blessed will have something to offer its workers who produce—and that something is recognition. The builder of important public works, the supervisor of a crew of flood fighters, or the negotiator of a crucial treaty does not lack incentive. He will develop his own momentum, without being driven by his superiors. There is little reason to be concerned about the productivity of this kind of bureaucrat.

The universal problem lies with those bureaulings who do not have any commitment to constructive achievement. These are the people who do not get any recognition directly for the agency's successes. They include some of the staff functionaries and so-called service workers who sup-

posedly support the producing members of the
bureau. Hanging around on the periphery, caressing their manuals, charts, and forms, they have no
reason to knock themselves out while the producers get the glory. Clusters of these slow-moving
onlookers can be found in nearly any agency. Unable to enjoy the limelight, they may tend to resent
those who do. And just to have some effect, even
though negative, they may work to frustrate the
goals of those others who have the opportunity and
the will to be creative. Fortunately, there are usually more dedicated service personnel to follow
them around and pick up the pieces.

My purpose is not only to help the various
souls in the labyrinth to find their way, but also to
provide citizens on the outside with some degree of
insight into the world of the bureau, to facilitate understanding of why bureaulings behave as they do.
Hopefully armed with this knowledge, those peek-
ing over the threshold in search of assistance may
know at least what to expect. First, they will not
expect too much. Second, they may recognize some
of the deadends in the maze, and not waste time in
probing these recesses. Third, some of the par-
lance of the inner sanctum will be deciphered to
permit communication across the mysterious
boundaries between bureauland and the surrounding territory.

These goals will be attempted by escorting the
reader through a book of seven parts: (1) an introduction which describes the bureaucratic environment and measures its merits and demerits; (2) the
ABC's of Bureaucracy, offering a preview in
twenty-six capsules; (3) guidelines for the bureaucratic recruit; (4) some words for members in the
middle echelons; (5) a look at the upper echelons,

where the chief executives and the politicians reside; (6) an examination of the places where the bureaucracy and the public meet; and (7) an epilogue, which pauses at the exit for recuperation.

To be honest, anybody who tries to explain such intricacies has to be a little irreverent, and therefore runs the risk of offending. After all, the institutions visited herein are venerable and often well treated by historians. Their beneficiaries are many. Their assailants have mostly fallen by the wayside. Why, then, should they not be left alone to do whatever they do? Because they need to be known better by the people whose lives they touch. If the journey through these pages makes even a slight improvement in this acquaintance, it will be worthwhile.

Chapter 2

the ABC's of Bureaucracy

The bureaucracy can be examined from many angles. Because of government's love for acronyms (CIA, FBI, FCC, HEW, HUD)—a curious verbal shortcut in an area where long channels are generally preferred—the alphabet may be used to present a diagnostic picture of the bureaucratic creature. The following pages therefore will attempt to draw the thing in a preliminary sketch, beginning with AUTHORITY and ending with ZIGZAGGING.

Authority

Regulatory expansion has turned the nation's capital into a prosperous city, even while the rest of the country suffered economic recession. Some analysts of government contend that power has increasingly been concentrated in Washington, D.C.

simply because the lower levels of government could not handle the economic and social demands of the people. If this is true, it must be at least partly attributable to the monopoly which the central government holds over the printing presses. The craving for authority abounds in all government centers. It is probably not much more plentiful in Washington than anywhere else, although the nation's capital does impose a strong gravitational pull on career bureaucrats.

Blanks

The Office of Management and Budget has estimated that American industry spends approximately 150 million man-hours each year in responding to federal questionnaires. Industry thus assists the government greatly in its efforts to control enterprise. Individual citizens have also been cooperative in helping their government to move its papers.

Nobody knows exactly how many forms the federal government puts out. Estimates vary widely. In a survey conducted by the Associated Press, for example, about ten thousand separate forms were discovered radiating from Washington, D.C., eliciting about 500 million responses each year. The Internal Revenue Service apparently ranks as the champion among forms processing agencies, with thirty-five hundred forms and about 120 million responses each year. The runner-up is the Department of Health, Education, and Welfare, which with slightly less than one thousand forms is able to extract approximately 175 million responses annually.

Of course, the federal government does not

have a monopoly on paperwork. Some of the states in the Union are highly competitive in this respect. The California government, for example, spends about $16 million a year for the printing of its forms, and an estimated $300 million a year to process them. While this is not very much in comparison with the $40 billion a year that the federal government pays to caress, disgorge, and store the approximately five million cubic feet of paper that is its annual product, the state makes a fair contribution to the flow of reports enjoyed by its citizens.

Controls

A century-old manual, designed for times when cleaning horse manure off the cobblestones was a prevalent governmental problem, can still be very effective in helping the bureau avoid a head-on collision with current challenges. When used properly it offers comfort to the multitude. The regulations—their writing, interpretation, observance, and enforcement—can occupy the time of many people. The more detailed the regulations are, the more work is created for everybody. Comprehensive edicts do call for comprehensive conformance. The most successful employees therefore tend to be those who devote much time to analyzing and memorizing and worshiping the manual. This kind of fervor in the ranks breeds necessarily some management preoccupation with trivia. The stuffing of the manual may also cause some hardening of the agency's arteries, but this is seldom fatal.

In the bureau world, the manual is the law. Its many enforcers see themselves as the sentries at the fences, keeping the flock from wandering. In their zeal they may be unconcerned about their own missteps but they do make a vital contribution to traditional officialism. They help to keep a lid on the disabling ferment of change. As the elite guard of officialism, the control agents never falter in their march through the paper tangle. They are fearless, but then they have nothing to fear.

Each level of government has its control agencies charged with maintaining surveillance over other units. Their purview may cover such fields as finance, personnel, and services. A control agency plays an essential role in relieving bureau chiefs of the discomfort of rejecting proposals from lower levels. Most of these agencies are more than willing to be the naysayers. Their success is measured by the rumbles of discontent among the restrained masses. The administrators can always pacify employees by pointing to the surveillant as the villain.

Enforcement of the manual's rigid concepts reduces discretion in the public servant's role and thereby brings him peace of mind. He can take comfort in sharing his responsibilities with the many who guide and review and approve his work. The hazards are minimal.

Dominion

Any sophisticated chief executive has to be a perceptive witness to the comings and goings of officialdom's flock. He must understand the manipulators and the enforcers and the snoopers and the nitpickers. They know their way through the profusion of regulations, and are therefore indispensable. Some of them have to be bridled to curb their predatory instincts but the majority comprises

well-disciplined, predictable performers dedicated
to maintenance of a stable course of government.

The chief executive who would seduce and exploit the bureau must first nourish its internal
needs. He must call to it from outside and not make
any disquieting attempts to enter. If it responds to
his overtures, it will do so as an integrated unit. In
fact, the bureaucracy could teach the rest of the
world something about unity, if it were so inclined.

Real changes in the structure of government
are difficult. Its footings are buried inaccessibly
under tough layers of bureaucratic fiber. Even to
gain insight into the entrenchments, the chief
executive has to work through agency hierarchy
who know the way in the outer passages of the
maze. The going is slow. His guides will lead him
only where they feel it is safe for him to enter. The
capable chief will not aspire to remold the system
drastically. He will see it clearly as a conglomer-
ate whose matrix is compromise, and he will respect its strength.

More than a few chief executives have been
frustrated by inability to get response from the bureaucracy. In their somewhat distorted view, procedures are too ponderous and the civil service is
overpopulated by an amorphous mass of lethargics. The leader who would dare to thin out the
ranks would be well advised to proceed with caution. Anybody who would cut the size of government has to face up to the consequences. The barriers are large. The legislative body will be
reluctant to reduce programs, and the employee
groups will also have something to say about it.
Nobody really wants to stop the spending machine.
The chief executive who is honestly frustrated by
this can find some consolation in that the ex-

panding scope of government promises a wider constituency.

Most governors, and even some presidents, are really good guys. In fact, being a good guy is one of the special requisites of the job. The chief's image has to be preserved. The people themselves demand it. Yet, in working through his insulating interpreters, the chief has no simple way to distinguish the real from the false. He must depend faithfully upon what his surrounders tell him, and upon what he can pick up by osmosis. Most civil servants will understand his situation and will be charitable toward him. Everybody knows that you have to help the chief look good—one of the rules of the game.

Exaltation

An official's appetite for prestige may be so voracious that it will never be sated by ordinary feeding. Various kinds of nourishment, in generous portions, may be vital to his survival.

Elevation of station in the bureaucratic community is recognized in exciting ways. Special attention is paid to admittance to the top staff meetings. This is a nearly infallible sign of ascendancy. Once inside the room, those so privileged will place emphasis on the seating arrangements. The officials at the main table are the anointed. The chairs along the wall, of course, are still better than being outside.

A seasoned bureaucrat likes to remind others of his status by such tactics as delaying his entrance into the meeting until all others have arrived. To assure proper timing, he can use a sentry at the door to check off the arrivals. When a meeting is to be held in his own premises—which he would usually prefer, for obvious effect—he habitually keeps his visitors waiting for a while before he enters.

Special attention should be given to the height of an executive's office furniture. For a successful meeting the leader should place himself at a level so that he can look down upon his visitors. It stimulates respect. Proper advantage can be secured by jacking up the desk and screwing the swivel chair to the top of its threads, thus gaining several inches in altitude over guests. To maintain dignity from such an elevated position, the chocks under the desk must be precisely leveled. Otherwise, pencils and toys may roll off onto the floor. This will be distracting. Another hazard is the overly efficient janitor who will lower the swivel chair to be helpful. The combination of high desk and low chair can cause a broken jaw.

A top-ranking bureaucrat is entitled to certain other prerogatives, like colored notepaper and a secretary with large buttocks. He has a right to screen and even exclude those who want to enter his office and to make his visitors wait in the reception area until he is ready to see them. Custom grants him a big office on the side of the building with the best scenery. It should have at least three windows and preferably more. An office with seven windows represents the ultimate in status and assures that practically all visitors will enter in awe.

Among the more elegant fixtures financed by public moneys are fish tanks, tinted glass, private pantries, recreation rooms, and sauna baths. A new high-level bureaucrat may be entitled by tradition to expend the equivalent of his first year's salary to improve his personal environment in this way.

The rules will spell out the grade of carpet corresponding to each executive rank. In some agencies there is no prohibition against use of personal funds to pay the difference in price for a better floor covering. While this may be a good investment, the wise officeholder will keep his surroundings noticeably less luxurious than those of his superior.

Status is displayed in many other ways: stationery with imprinted rank; autographed photographs of dignitaries; color-coded DO-NOT-DISTURB signs; overstuffed furniture; marble-topped tables on oriental rugs; waiting rooms with free ghostwritten literature; private conference rooms; and a staff of executive assistants to fetch coffee and cigars.

Another unfailing clue is the number of in-baskets and out-baskets in the office. A man who has a full set in his secretary's office as well as his own is undoubtedly a few rungs above the pack. The number of boxes in each set is a giveaway. A complete set might have such labels as IN, OUT, HOLD, REFERENCE, FILE, RECYCLE, SHRED, SIGNATURE, EXPEDITE, and PRIORITY. The ten-basket bureaucrat is a peculiarly impressive product of the system.

The prize which stimulates a maximum of executive delight is the hot line. To be effective it must be given to only a chosen few. Basically a hot line is nothing more than a series of wires terminating in a button-studded console in the boss's office and in alarm devices in the offices of his subordinates. Most are designed to be two-way communication devices, but in usual practice the alarm is sounded only in a downward direction. The executive who wants to exploit the full potential of the mechanism will check the daily calendars of his subordinates and will arrange to trigger the alarm at the height of their meetings. He will want them to be reminded of his station at regular intervals, varying his timing only enough to keep them alert. To hone a fine edge on the nerves of a subordinate, the hot-line signal should have a high-frequency tone. In fact, it should be shrill.

Fanfare

Ceremony is food for the soul of the bureaucrat. Lovers of ritual have been known to cause painful injuries in their elbowing rush to grab the gladhand. Aside from the therapeutic advantages, there are other good reasons to encourage this attention to celebration. Common statesmanship requires it. But not everybody should be allowed to participate. A celebrity will expect to be entertained by only the highest of rank. The bureaucrat must therefore arrange his itinerary so that nobody has to substitute for him on ceremonial occasions. He will insist that all inquiries from Very Important Persons be referred to him. Otherwise, he can explain, agency image and policy could hardly be consistent. His subordinates will understand.

Other factors being equal, the VIP himself would prefer to associate with another VIP, preferably one of higher rank. Ceremonial dedications offer ideal opportunity for such intercourse. They have limitless potential. Any project can be divided into many components. A testimonial program can be scheduled for each facility as it is completed, spreading these rites over several years to achieve the optimum effect. The public will always come to see the performers.

Some of the most conscientious efforts of gov-

ernment go into planning these spectacles. Much
manpower must be diverted from lower priorities
to assure success. Committees must be established
for public relations, entertainment, finance, and
site preparation. Committeemen for the cere-
monies must give attention to a multitude of necessary services. Platforms and bleachers must be
constructed; public address systems must be installed; souvenir programs and banners and straw
hats have to be stocked; parking lots and parade
grounds must be graded; booths need to be erected
for sale of soft drinks, popcorn, and cotton candy;
and chemical toilets have to be placed at strategic
locations throughout the ceremonial area. The
grandstand will be designed to give an unob-
structed view of the performers.

A prominent place on the platform is precious.
Feelings can be irreparably damaged if somebody
deserving is overlooked. A promising advancement in ceremonial techniques which still has not
been fully exploited involves the designing of
grandstands with various levels to differentiate
status, like the loges and balconies in a theater. But
the vertical dimensions are difficult to set. Much
remains to be done to perfect the devices for maxi-
mizing ritual benefits. No matter what is done,
favors will still be traded for a place on the re-
viewing stand. This is valuable currency.

Any well-planned ceremony will leave behind
a bronze plaque of some kind lauding the officials
who performed at the unveiling. The order of rank
on these plaques takes a lot of calculation, and not
infrequently more than a modicum of conspiracy.

Glorification

An honest bureaucrat with genuine executive

ability may find limited financial rewards in government service. Some incentive must be substituted for the money which he would have earned if he had chosen to work instead for General Motors or Standard Oil or Universal Amalgamated Industries. A generally accepted satisfier is the homage which can be expected from lower civil servants and from the public at large. The importance of this should not be underestimated in seeking an understanding of what makes some bureaucrats tick.

Friendly media may take care of the bureaucrat's image among the general citizenry, but within his bailiwick he is largely on his own, among fellow employees who know him too well to be deceived. Still, most of them will recognize his special needs. An executive who is feeling depressed is entitled to deference. If he feels inadequate he deserves to be praised. His best self-administered therapy is to make an example of somebody, to assert his authority. A subordinate can be called in and accused of violating the rules. Nearly any underling will be an adequate target. A superior bureaucrat can do this easily, since any rule is subject to interpretation. There is no need to give the subordinate an opportunity for rebuttal or defense. If he is properly trained he will accept a reprimand without argument. He will not be so inconsiderate as to deny his superior one little salute.

Hustings

Some bureaucrats try to minimize their exposure to politicians, for fear that they will be infected by contact. Actually, the only contagion that might be communicated would be an intense yearning for votes. Most bureaucrats do not have to

worry about this kind of affliction. They are lucky
enough to be immune from election fever. The chief
executive's appointees, whose fortunes rise and
fall with the condition of their benefactor at the
polls, are in a different category. They can be excused if they show some nervousness about the
wishes of the electorate.

Bureaucrats cannot really escape association
with politicians. They should therefore try harder
to understand them. The elected representatives of
the people do not spend all their time in pursuit of
women, drink, and publicity. Most of them work
very hard and have sincere desires to be of service.

Of course, the people must be convinced that
they are getting their money's worth. A politician
hit by the shattering force of the vote can collapse
and be unmourned, while bureaulings wade care-
free through the debris.

The bureaucrat should be proficient in dis-
pensing the wealth of others. By dealing in the
earnings of the industrious and redistributing
these confiscations to the most conspicuous needy,
the images of the government and of its practi-
tioners can be profitably brightened. Tax col-
lecting and other unappreciated governmental
duties are assigned to anonymous underlings who
do not need the love of the populace. On the other
hand, any manifestation of officialdom's generosity should be made to flow from the fingers of its
exposed elite.

Indolents

In some places, culls would be dumped as
worthless. In bureauland the judgment is not so
harsh. Its system protects them and tolerates their

defects. It understands the resentment that irreversible typecasting may engender. The relegation is discomforting for a few. Those unable to assimilate the behavioral norms may tend to confuse conformity with prostitution, especially if they have been sidetracked for proclamation of their superiority over their superiors. Though not easily separated from their attitudes, they can still serve. They invariably have firm anchorages and can lend stability by remaining unmoved in any dynamic situation.

Therefore, unless a bureauling is a real menace, he or she can be surplus and be conveniently overlooked. Such employees provide balance in an organization. Some of them are nice people, tolerable fixtures in the system. With all their faults, these special members of the bureaucratic community still can make their marks. They stand just as firmly against disruptive progress as does anybody in the institution.

Jobbers

The employee with the most comfortable home in the bureaulands may be the staff analyst who builds his own little kingdom, protected by the weight of the manual. Adjusted to a fine tuning, this will require an alliance with the custodian of the manual and will involve an exclusive assignment such as the processing of a certain government form. The possessors of such jobs may call themselves coordinators or expediters. Those who wait for their service may give them other labels. Typically this is a one-employee operation. The processor of the form must handle everything personally without substitutes or assistants. This will assure that he has unchallenged jurisdiction. He must insist that nobody else be allowed to touch his documents. His files are not to be shared with anybody. This is the only way that he can guarantee the highest degree of expertise.

This single-purpose specialist is a lightweight in comparison with the broad-gauged jobber who deals in data traffic throughout the bureau. Since the government machinery runs on information, a dispenser of this fuel occupies an envied position. The machine cannot be operated without him. To impress others with the importance of his role, he should issue his data in measured amounts. A dealer in informational tidbits will withhold his stuff until he is assured of the best return on his investment. This will come from somebody who cannot do without it.

The specialist in collection and disbursement of information may not have much interest in its end use. Characteristically he will be much more concerned about its value in bartering for advantage. The dependency of others is assured as long as the interlocking bits of data are not put on the table at the same time. By causing all essential channels of communication to flow through him, he can deprive others of a full understanding of problems. As long as he is the only one who is not confused, he will remain in control.

In shouldering the burden of coordination the data keeper performs a service which is widely appreciated by employees who are discomforted by responsibility. Many bureaulings do not want the obligations that arise from data possession. However, once in a while some aspiring upstart will demand a more generous rationing of the information coming to him. If he cannot be suppressed or rejected, room may have to be made for another jobber in the organization. One more will not make much difference.

Kingpins

The inhabitants of bureauland are accustomed to receiving new leaders from time to time. Changing of command in the labyrinth is likely to be met by choruses of shrugs and yawns. Nobody expects bureaucratic newcomers to have truly measurable impact. These transients are tolerated as long as they leave the institution intact. The prescribed behavior for these nomadic administrators includes acceptance of the anchored positions and functions in the labyrinth. To avoid adverse reactions, the appointee who has come to stay for a while must keep his hands off the machinery. The scope and the duration of the custodianship may depend as much on bureaucratic acceptance as on the wishes of the chief executive.

The custodian who devotes himself to hierarchical responsiveness and leaves the bureau to run itself can enjoy a peaceful term in office. By staying above ordinary decision making he will have wide purview with ample time to ponder. From his elevated chair he will be able to survey the activities of lesser overseers, to analyze their meanderings, and to offer generous commentary without the burden of commitment. Little more will be expected of him by his subordinates.

Meditation helps to insulate the executive from those who make demands upon him. Behind the meditative curtain he can relax and avoid worrying about the disgorgings of the paper mill. Preferably this should not be practiced in a conspicuous way. Some meditators are regarded as peculiar.

Loyalists

No government office would achieve its full potential without a dedicated yes-man or two. These extreme loyalists provide stability to an organization in important ways. They are predictable. They can be counted on to support the management whether right or wrong. An executive who suffers anxieties can get no better therapy than to encircle himself with yes-men. They will never be so graceless as to present him with options that force him into agonizing decisions. And if somehow he makes an apparent mistake on his own, his loyal and sympathetic subordinates can help him dismiss it or rationalize it into a success.

Yes-men are also handy scapegoats and targets of abuse. The boss can stamp on them to his heart's content. He will never hear their whimpers. Their protests will be subtle and silent, like chewing gum stuck in the cracks in the plaster, or torn-out cloth towels in the restrooms, or spit and trash on the stairways.

Bureaucratic institutions offer expansive opportunities to people who can and will fit themselves into a precisely organized structure. Like the pieces in a jigsaw puzzle they must interlock in harmony with their neighbors in the system. The developing bureaucrat must eschew individualism as he settles into his niche. Once he is ensconced he should memorize the basic principles of the institution.

Any prudent subordinate will research the attitudes and the desires of the management so that his own activities will vibrate in tune with hierarchical expectations. From his stressful and perhaps precarious perch the top man will be soothed by the voices of those who echo his opinions and cheer his pronouncements. Underlings who engage in such deification will be looked upon benevolently. An aspiring bureaucrat who shapes himself in the image of his boss will enjoy immediate advantage. He should not be alarmed if he finds that others are doing the same thing. He just has to work harder at being a better impersonator. A top executive will find comfort in being surrounded by a hundred likenesses of himself. The supporting players in the drama must rehearse their lines until they can project with sincerity. The cultivation of rapport in the executive chambers requires a credible display of servitude.

Majorettes

In most corners of advanced society, women historically established their image as weak and dependent. The masculine ego was caressed into assuming the appearance of dominance. Despite the recent advances in women's liberation, the relationship is still prevalent. In playing this traditional role, the male in officialdom must be sensitive to the currents of feeling generated by the female governmental contingent. Alone or in coalition, they are not ordinary women. Distaff members of the bureaucracy are a special kind that bear careful watching. Their influence in the power structure has been known to shake up more than a few unwary civil servants.

Since the purportedly dominant male ego may

not encourage the girls to wear their chevrons openly, many of their channels are run underground where their communications flow freely to every corner of the government edifice. In fact, the female ententes between political and bureaucratic sectors are likely to be stronger and more productive than most alliances forged by men. The males of bureauland tend to segregate into horizontal bands, insulated from vertical communication. Only an exceptional boss can get feedback all the way from the bottom. This is not so with the ladies. Their proclivity for oral exchange helps them to hear their sisters' whispers at all levels. The sorority's free access throughout the labyrinth is used in various ways. Perhaps fortunately for the male hierarchy, most of the girls do not really want to depose them. Their silent power is applied to better advantage, while the men are left with the ulcers.

Naysaying and Nit-picking

The staff reviewer serves a useful purpose. While he will be reluctant to make a sustaining effort to get a thing done, his meticulous examination of any subject laid before him assures that ideas will not explode prematurely. This specialist can be used to counter the articulate spokesman who advances proposals often just to get attention. Half-baked suggestions must be scrutinized and the nit-picker is just the one to do it. He seldom has ideas of his own but he knows how to shred the work of others.

Although many employees will embrace the rules as protection against responsibility, a nonconformist minority will plead for more freedom of action. The staff enforcers must give such resistance close attention. They have to be the missionaries who propagate the faith.

A manager's job in government is done with these many helpers. In a climate set to restrain the venturesome, the manual's caretakers keep everybody else in line. Nobody has to worry about mistakes filtering through the many layers of review. The ubiquitous manual-toters will massage the hell out of everything. They appreciate the value of intrastaff cooperation in ruling the lives of those on the production line. The opportunity and the desire for such domination are most acute in the central headquarters. There the staff reviewers try to respond to the public conception of the civil servant as a parasite. Some of them have contributed significantly to that image.

A favorite pitch of the red-tape spinner is that full-scale surveillance is required to prevent abuses. Of course, to a large extent postauditing would serve the purpose. But this alone offers less opportunity for control. What the watchdogs demand instead is authority of approval before an action can take place. By insisting on this role they regulate the flow of work. For insurance there is built into the system all the methodology to provide that each producer has at least three of these nonproducers watching him to see that he follows the rules and accounts for every coin. It works, of course. There is seldom any scandal involving civil service employees. And it keeps the staff proceduralists off the welfare rolls.

Overseeing

To motivate the government forces, an assortment of levers is essential. While an overseer can be moved by power and homage, the little fellows under his rule are more likely to be influenced by the demands of group membership. A paper processor who accelerates outflow may please neither his supervisor nor his associates. The only reward may be ostracism, unless he can be persuaded to moderate his work pace so that the expansionary objectives of the bureau are not subverted. He must be made aware of the hazards of overproduction. For one thing he must realize that fast work can deprive the group of overtime pay. The idea of work measurement is repugnant to most subordinates. Through an unofficial pact they usually adopt their own range of acceptable output. The resultant level of performance for the group as a whole will be a compromise that provides comfortable working conditions.

Perpetuation

Bureaudom is composed of well-guarded protectorates, with built-in mechanisms for perpetuation. To thrive and endure, accountants need more accounts, statisticians need more statistics, dispensers of funds need more recipients, and the control agents need a bigger manual. Expansion generates more jobs, more pay, and higher seniority for those who came first.

There is a strong incentive to establish greater quantities of everything that makes the system rotate, to develop more programs and to extend programs that are not needed any longer. The continuation of long-standing activities is the easiest and most popular way to perpetuate. This is particularly attractive when a contribution of federal funds is involved. Nobody in his right mind is likely to volunteer a reduction or elimination of work funded by the Treasury. Everybody knows that if he does not take it somebody else will grab it.

Perpetuation of bureaucracy and the bureaucratic species is a primary obligation of each member of the institution. Most employees fulfill this naturally and without urging. Those who dedicate themselves consciously to this mission will see clearly their essential place in the defense of civilized order. Without bureaucracy there would be no world as we know it today. Any aware citizen would judge this to be a bleak prospect indeed.

Critics have demanded explanation of the statistical indication that governments at all levels have been growing at a rate several times that of the population growth. This is undoubtedly attributable to the rapid multiplication of problems as government becomes more sophisticated. As the people turn more and more to their government to take care of them, they have to expect bureaucratic armies to multiply. The growth has to be exponential simply because each problem creates attendant problems which must be processed.

Quorum

Committees beget committees and in their proliferation undoubtedly do much good. There are many advantages in collective consideration of an idea. The group can provide a blended input from a wide spectrum of experience and philosophy. Problems can be dissected and examined exhaustively. Through cross-fertilization of diverse viewpoints whole new ideas may be born, and then dissected and examined in turn.

Committees may even be good for the participants. By sharing in discussion they will develop a
feeling of belonging, a spirit of comradeship. Also,
the opportunity to size up the other fellow offers
some leverage in case of future conflict. Group
membership engenders pride in participation and
perhaps even in accomplishment once in a while.
The committeeman's traditional right to be heard is
especially sweet tonic for the one to whom nobody
normally would be inclined to listen.

Deliberation in concert can serve to glue together the fragments of authority in an agency. Although it may be a degradable adhesive, sometimes it will last long enough to promote a decision.
Certainly there are other ways to provide a climate for action, such as strengthening the line organization, but committees are much easier to establish. Moreover, the route via group meditation
may be safer to travel. It detours around strong
managers who may be inclined to pursue their
goals too vigorously. Their straight path may be
productive, but this must be balanced against the
hazards of concentrating power in the hands of the
very able.

Very few institutional components contribute
as much to stability and continuity as does the
committee. It has an intrinsic resistance to disruptive stimulus and to precipitous action. For this, it
enjoys widespread popularity.

Reciprocity

Reciprocity, a favorite sport in some legislative bodies, is also played with enthusiasm at bureaucratic levels. As a handy everyday tool, backscratching enhances relationships in many ways

and in many quarters. Whether applied vertically or horizontally, it seldom fails to yield therapeutic results.

Pork-barreling or logrolling or back-scratching—whatever it may be called—can be a particularly effective catalyst in a standing committee, where proposals of special interest to one committeeman can be treated generously by the others at the table with a view toward sympathetic handling of their own pet issues at subsequent meetings. Committeemen often trade favors without open negotiation. Harmony springs from an unvoiced understanding.

Subjugation

Success in the bureaucratic world is measured in various ways. Self-preservation is basic, but the ability to branch out and subjugate others clearly separates the stars from the bit players. The achieved dominance does not have to show on the organization chart. Subordinates of others are fair game, and their subjugation can be just as real whether the official records show it or not.

Mastery of the art of subjugation is markedly facilitated if the dominator-in-training is naturally inclined to act the bully. Even with this inherent advantage, many techniques must still be learned. Underlying most of these is the premise that subordinates will be kept on a short rein. They should be questioned frequently about what they have done, what they are doing, and what they plan to do. They should be called in often for interrogation on short notice. Written reports should be demanded with tight deadlines, and then sent back for repeated revision until they are fully reflective of management views. Subordinates should be forced to plead for their vacations, and to call in at regular intervals while they are away. After all this, some underlings will still be unresponsive. The subjugator's work is never done.

Coercion should not be applied to such an extent that it blackens the dominator's image or diverts the subordinate out of the bureaucratic mainstream. A purpose of the subjugation is to ensure compliance with institutional norms, not to oppress the masses unduly. Those who acquiesce should be treated gently.

Under normal conditions, aggressors who strive to increase their following should be given liberal encouragement. This assumes, of course, that the subjugator is a loyal bureaucrat who will faithfully instill in his subjects all the fine principles of the institution. In this good cause he is deserving of a maximum of support.

In a broader sense, the aims of subjugation extend to all corners of the land. The whole populace is conditioned to accept the rules and forms and guidance of the bureaucracy. In countries where these have not been respected, governments and societies have been transitory. Stability can only derive from a firm bureaucracy.

Some national leaders have tried to subjugate the bureaucracy itself. Practically all such attempts have failed.

Takeover

Increased authority is often most easily achieved by increasing the number of subordinates. Of course, as more people are added, the indifference of subordinates to supervisors may also

increase—but not necessarily in the same proportion. The bureaucrat seeking to enlarge his influence will usually have to justify enlarged programs if he wants more employees under his
purview. This means carving off chunks of the territory of other bureaucrats and thus runs some risk
of retaliation. A real takeover artist, however, will
not be deterred by this prospect. He will be willing
to fight for more than his share of the budget, more
than his share of subordinates, and more than his
share of recognition.

In marking the territorial boundaries of the
agency, its leaders must be daringly liberal. Some
knowledge of military tactics can be helpful in expanding the frontiers and in guarding them against
attack. The struggle requires a large commitment
of the bureau's resources. The expense is justified,
since neighboring bureaus otherwise could freely
overrun the territory and put the home army out of
business. Any self-respecting bureaucracy will respond to such a threat to its survival, even though
it may be unresponsive to nearly everything else.

Upkeep

The bureau's people have their mettle tested
annually in the planning of expenditures. During a
year of gestation the governmental budget devel-
ops into an exquisite complex of paperwork. To
facilitate its interpretation it must be accompanied by a myriad of charts and analytical treatises. Although their preparation is time-con-
suming, they are essential to the movement of the
budget through the channels to become a control
device.

Since the budget has a long route to travel

through the labyrinth, its supporting literature will be well read by a multitude. A few of these readers are likely to understand it. Some cynics see a danger in this. They contend that an understandable budget would soon be cut to ribbons, thus threatening the very roots of bureaucracy. Such cynicism is certainly unwarranted. The system's anchorages are much stronger than that.

A full-fledged bureaucrat must be a vigorous spokesman for the programs of his agency. He will promote them with enthusiasm and do everything that he can to assure their expansion. Enlargement of budgeted activities will be always on his mind. This is how the bureaucrat makes his mark, not by just sustaining the status quo but by building layers and layers of new functions and nailing them down with the stimulated support of new or enlarged constituencies. While innovation is frowned upon if it does violence to the Manual, it will be lauded if it can be translated into a broadening of the sphere of influence of the agency and an enhancement of the images of its leaders.

The heads of some government agencies feel that their future and the futures of their constituencies will be bright only if they press the legislative bodies for more money. They not only cry for larger budgets, but they also will demonstrate their ability to spend once the funds are granted. Nobody can afford to arrive at the end of the fiscal year with part of his budget unspent. Such miscalculation would undoubtedly be used against him in the drafting of future budgets. An administrator with a declining budget suffers a stigma that is especially unpleasant. Declining budgets are synonymous with declining careers. Legislators have a clear insight into this bureaucratic problem and may be inclined to spare the bureaus such embarrassment. Traditionally they have been willing to guarantee the continuity of any established government program that is even half justified, and they will often be receptive to proposals for enlargement or for entirely new functions.

Vernacular

Knowledge of the system's language is helpful in finding the way through the bureaucratic underbrush. The most common jargon serves to reduce visibility, using snowy words for budgeting unneeded programs, weasel words for reporting progress on activities that have not progressed, and soapy words for erasing errors. The glossary is revealing, like a lamp in the shadows.

Most of the jargon of the bureau is developed to be usable only within the institutional confines. It facilitates understanding among bureaucrats but loses some of its value outside the walls. The language has to be learned the hard way. Published compilations of words and phraseology are rare. Their existence would present a hazard to the quiet functioning of the system. To be most effective the special terminology must remain the exclusive property of the bureau.

The bureaucratic asylum is being attacked from some quarters to open its walls to public scrutiny. Some observers resent the use of a special language within the institution and insist that it be deciphered for the benefit of outsiders. What they should realize is that verbalization in the proprietary tongue facilitates comprehensive commentary. Without this, channels would surely be choked by common words that could be found in any dictionary. The agency's vernacular is more than a convenient communicative device. It is one of the important assets that give permanency to the bureaucracy. No other justification need be offered for its existence.

Wordcraft

Few bureaucrats progress far in the labyrinth without the ability to gush plenty of words. Any acceptable action must be preceded by comprehensive deliberation. To provide for participation by a maximum of interested parties, oral and written exchanges should be profuse. Any course that eventually may be adopted must be subjected to inspection, analysis, and reporting. This scrutiny will instill caution in action-oriented workers and impress upon them the consequences of moving without proper justification. Those who attack their work energetically should be required to explain why they do what they do, and why they have rejected alternative courses—including doing nothing. Otherwise those with unusual initiative would be striding out in their own directions, in the interest of achievement without regard for impact.

To obtain maximum benefit from institutional membership the bureaucrat must convert simplicities into fully developed intricacies. To ensure that a statement will be defensible in the future, one should include ample qualifying terms and tentative clauses. While a speaker's basic message may be simple, he should never communicate it without extensive examination of lateral and longitudinal relativities. The merits and demerits of alternative themes should be explored and correlated so that all aspects are laid out to enable listeners to reach their own conclusions.

An executive proficient in the communicative arts usually will not feel compelled to bring his words to sharp focus. He will appreciate the hazards of precipitous commitments. As long as the slightest bit of information remains to be examined, he is not under much obligation to be conclusive. To avoid being misunderstood the sender of information should therefore be reasonably equivocal. An explicit message allows no room to maneuver. Liberal insertion of escape clauses is essential to accommodate the bias of the receiver. Indefinite modifiers help to avoid impressions of dogmatism. Most observers will appreciate a communicator who concedes that he does not know everything. By recognizing that anything can have more than one interpretation, he will be seen as openminded.

Xerocopiers

Those copying machines are wonderful. No office can afford to be without one. There is no way to calculate the immense benefits that they have brought to the bureaucracy. They have helped everybody to be busier. Executives have more to read, clerks have more paper to process, and auditors who monitor machine usage have enjoyed stimulation bordering on the erotic.

The great gushing of paper is essential. With so many people involved in each activity, information must flow. The xerocopy machine has enabled an acceleration of wordage rates beyond the fondest of bureaucratic hopes just a few years ago. If one high-speed device is provided for each two hundred employees, on the average, most of the needs of a modern government office can be satisfied.

Xerocopyism has opened new horizons for

those bent on control. With more and more copies going to more and more desks, anybody is prepared to intervene in the province of his neighbor. Speed of reproduction has enabled easy interception and distribution of anything flowing in the channels. A favorite maneuver of the system's spies is to ambush memoranda from an enemy camp and to sneak quick xerocopies for collaborators. This practice has led to countermeasures. Machines are locked and unlocked by appointed custodians, or sentries are posted to police the operation, or special messengers are detailed to circumvent the office mail routes. All of this creates more jobs and thus gives sustenance to the system.

Yes-Machines

Electronic data processing has opened up important opportunities for protection and extension of bureaucracy. In recognition of this, vast quantities of money are being spent on computer software and hardware. Each of the components and subcomponents is designed to be a dependent part of a complex package which can receive and hold the data wealth of the bureau. The necessary interlocking assures that what is done will not be easily undone. An obligation to posterity is thus fulfilled.

Full attention has been given to data processing requirements in practically all government agencies. For many years the administrations and the legislative bodies have conducted comprehensive studies and have published many reports on computer applications. As a matter of fact, the compilation and analysis of statistics for these reports and their appendices have contributed significantly to the governmental workload.

Most legislators are interested in the control of data processing. Lengthy hearings by their various committees may actually succeed in slowing the rising cost of machine operation in government units. Of course, funding for data purposes in the law-making institution itself has been escalating. Committees on legislative economies have taken note of this and have augmented their own budgets so that the problem can be properly analyzed.

As the inhabitants of bureauland become better adjusted to the computerized arrangement of their lives, they undoubtedly will grow to appreciate electronic manipulation almost as much as do the personnel who service the machines and depend on them for livelihood. There is every reason to expect that, as these human adjustments are made, organizational barriers will dissolve and all hands will clasp to push the buttons together.

Of course, the benefits must be shared with the public at large. Those bureaucrats knowledgeable of computer behavior offer in chorus that government cannot spread its purview much further without enlarged automatic data processing capacity. They see myriad opportunities for extending computer regulation into every home. Already the memories of thousands and thousands of computers contain data enough for printouts to keep all government workers reading continuously without relief. The collection of computerized data for storage in a national depository is well advanced and busily drawing from millions of households. Information is available on every citizen. Many agencies are actively engaged in providing this service and, if they ever get coordinated, surveillance of the people's lives can be optimized to a high degree.

Zigzagging

A cardinal rule of the expert executive is to zig-zag to present a difficult target. The bureaucrat who hopes to weather the storms must spend much of his time plotting his strategies and assessing the vulnerability of each adversary. To keep them guessing he must always have a package of alternatives. Sometimes when everybody expects him to turn to the left he should turn to the right. An unpredictable behavioral pattern is a valuable defense.

Richard Nixon was a primary example of a zig-zagger in action. During his last months in the presidency he did everything that he could do to shake the wolves off his tail. His bobbing and weaving and hiding are now part of history. Almost to the bitter end he expected that somehow he would shake them loose. He was nearly crafty enough to pull it off but there were just too many pulling for all they were worth to tear him down. He zigged and he zagged but in the end he went down.

Those in pursuit of the zigzagger must remember that the trapped prey may have sharp teeth. The wise pursuer will sometimes leave an exit open rather than run the risk of being wounded himself. After a few narrow escapes the zigzagger may become weary. That's the time to stamp him into submission.

Chapter 3

the Entry-Level Bureaucrat

Entering

People who aspire to even the most modest posts in the labyrinth must allow themselves to be tested before gaining admission. The examinations used to measure their qualifications run a gamut, depending upon the position desired, the agency doing the testing, and the intensity of the competition. There are oral interviews and written tests, and sometimes there are combinations of both. In some cases, acceptance or rejection is determined solely by rating the experience record of the candidate.

Nearly any library or bookstore carries a supply of books telling how to take civil service exams. If you know the right people, you can even get hold of copies of old tests, along with the answers. And that brings us to an important point. You have to give the right answers, the responses that the examiners want to hear. Even before crossing the threshold you must demonstrate that you have learned this first lesson in conformance.

Indoctrination

No better advice could be given the novice bureaucrat than to study the skillful government professionals at work. He will be fascinated by their large repertoires of precisely executed moves. Whether he aspires to emulate them or not, he will be better prepared to counter their thrusts and to survive in the bureaucratic tailwash.

On those occasions when the veteran bureaucrat chooses to expose himself to the scrutiny of management, he may appear to be in productive motion. The reports which he generates may be saturated with impressive generalizations that suggest vibrant progress. He will be emphatic, projecting sincerity even when delivering material of little substance. He knows that he will be remembered more for appearance than for the quality of his product. Even on a routine day of circulation in the maze he will emit flashes of contributory dynamics whenever within view of a high observer.

By following such exemplary behavior, nearly anybody can succeed as a bureaucratic resident. Keeping a low profile, though, can also be effective. Knowing his limitations and staying within them, the resident can avoid being a threat to anybody. Once he makes clear that he knows his place, he will have passed probation. Nobody will expect him to display the noise and the brightness that go with command. To anchor himself comfortably, he should preferably study some segment of the proprietary knowledge in the bureau. The more narrowly specialized this is, the better. By memorizing the information and repeating the exercises, the aspirant can become known as a specialist. This makes him a link in the chain on which others depend. By doing his little task over and over again, he inspires trust and disturbs nobody. His license to do his thing is likely to go unchallenged, particularly if his thing is monotonous and unattractive.

Knowing the Rules

One of the vitals of the control system is the Manual, a comprehensive collection of laws, regulations, and prohibitions that delineate each inch of allowable movement for the total multitude of public servants in the province. Its purposes include the elimination of discretion and the minimization of independent action. Some call it the Bible, and in this sense its religion is uniformity.

The sheer size of the Manual guarantees inflexibility and all the natural comforts that go with it. While the dynamics of community needs might call for some changes in the rules, they will come slowly. Sections are added from time to time but deletions are far apart. Over the scores of years, therefore, overlaps have been allowed to enter. They assure that nothing is left uncovered. The laminations of rules, like new shingles laid over old, provide mildewy impermeability to the attack of the elements.

To be versed in the essential procedures, a bureaucrat-in-training must study hundreds of pages such as the following, taken directly from an existing manual:

FORMS CONTROL

7700

RESPONSIBILITY (Rev. Apr/73)

7710

The Management Analysis Office is responsible for a Department forms management program.

DEFINITION OF A FORM (New, Dec/61)

7720

A form is any piece of paper containing information, printed or otherwise reproduced, with blank spaces left for entry of additional data or information. Forms include letterheads, letters, memoranda, envelopes, route slips, and mailing tags.

ASSIGNMENT OF FORM NUMBERS (Rev. Apr/73)

7730

Numbers are assigned to   forms by the Management Analysis Office. All new forms and revisions must be submitted to this office for approval before they are numbered. Reprinting of an additional supply of an existing form with no change in the form will not be regarded as a form revision; however, the order must be approved by the Management Analysis Office.

EXCEPTED FORMS (Rev. May/65; Renum. Apr/73)

7731

Forms intended for use to collect data for a one-time project or survey are excepted from the form numbering requirement. Indicate this fact on the printing requisition. Excepted forms should still comply with minimum standards expressed in   Section 7760.

FORMS FILE (Rev. Apr/73)

A file, in numerical order, consisting of one copy of each form used in the Department, will be maintained by the Management Analysis Office. Two copies of each new, revised or rerun form are to be sent to the Management Analysis Office by the Duplicating Unit as soon as a form is reproduced. If the form is printed, two copies are to be sent by the Purchasing and Stores Unit as soon as the form is received from the Printing Plant. The number of copies reproduced, the initiating organization unit, and the date of reproduction are to be shown by pencil notation on one of the two copies sent to the Management Analysis Office.

CONSULTATION ON REQUEST (Rev. Apr/73)

Consultation regarding forms design, use and method of reproduction may be had by calling the Management Analysis Office.

MINIMUM FORM STANDARDS (Rev. Apr/73)

Forms must meet certain minimum requirements.

a. Each form must have a letterhead or other appropriate identification showing the State , The Agency, and the name of the Department. If the form is to be restricted to the use of one division, district or branch, its name may also be shown on the letterhead.

b. Each form must show a title or heading. The title should indicate the functional use of the form.

c. If the form may be used for key punching or other data processing procedures, the layout should be reviewed by the Division of Computer Systems before printing.

d. Forms will show position titles rather than names of individuals.

A primary rule embodied in the Manual's many chapters is that any modification in policy or procedures must result from concerted action. An individual is not empowered to change direction by himself. The alteration of bureaucratic course therefore requires comprehensive preparation. The Manual itself is a collection of decisions made in advance, necessarily without the facts on specific situations. The circumstances which develop must be drastically different from what the Manualists envisioned if a proposed revision is to stand a chance. A common motive must exist to bring collaborators together, such as defense against an outsider's challenge or preservation of the bureaucracy itself. Short of such a powerful incentive, a major shift in direction is unlikely.

Most members of the order accept the rules of standard conduct and participate willingly in the disciplined ritualism that goes with them. The institution's masses find comfort in belonging. The emotional ointment of togetherness compensates for the impersonal detachment required of the civil servant in dealing with citizen clients, where feelings must be subordinated to the broader purposes of the law.

Generally, a new rule will be followed as obediently as an old one. For example, at a state government building in California a new emergency alarm and public address system was installed. A directive to all employees announced that in the event of an emergency a siren signal would be sounded throughout the building for three continuous minutes and would then be followed by a voice message from the command post. Presumably bureaulings were expected to wait patiently for three minutes until the siren's howling stopped before they could be informed about the crisis. Questions did arise as to how to cope with a two-minute emergency such as a bomb with a short fuse. However, in the absence of any further instruction, well-disciplined bureaulings will wait the full three minutes before scrambling.

Sometimes rules will allow room for interpretation. As an example, there was a graphics unit in one agency which was required frequently to do photographic and exhibit work for the hierarchy and the hierarchy's friends, and always to hide the cost in the overhead account. After being submerged by requests for such favors, the supervisors in the unit decided to abide by the rules and keep records on such expenses. When they had accumulated enough to have an impact they made the accounts available to auditors, legislators, and the media. While they thus complied with the rules for proper accounting, they violated an even more sacred rule against disclosures of bureau business outside the bureau. It is not a recommended way to straighten out the bosses, even though the chortling in this graphics unit continued for a long time.

Some of the labyrinth's overseers have little patience with subordinates who would disturb the peace of bureaudom. In their eyes, conformance may measure higher than invention. Sometimes an underling dare not look too good, lest some overseer would feel threatened. Outstanding performance may have to be displayed in low key to avoid rumpling security blankets at high level. The bureaucratic aspirant who dares to innovate must expect his ventures to be severely scrutinized. A much safer way to make a mark in the bureaucracy is to serve in the reinforcement of the Manual. Innovation has its place in science and music, but in the bureaucracy it is too conspicuous and un-settling. Maintenance of the status quo gives com-fort to those whose talents and ambitions are limited and who are satisfied with the plateau on which they are resting. They don't want anybody tampering with the perquisites that they have accumulated over the years.

Knowing the Language

Circuitous verbalizing is vital to the process of pondering decisions and contemplating uncer-tainties. This is a talent which must be cultivated. The beginning bureaucrat should keep his own list of terms and add to it as he absorbs the utterances of the system's veterans. He should suspend the paper flow momentarily from time to time and examine the content for choice phrases to augment his verbal armament. As he gains profi-ciency in speaking the bureaucratic tongue, he will make wider and wider use of proprietary words which have meaning only within the system. This will stimulate his sense of belonging and provide him protective insulation against inhabitants of the outside world. These words licensed for use in the bureau do facilitate common understandings with a minimum of commitment. Regular use of accepted communicative guidelines will help in finding the way up the institutional stairs.

The language of the labyrinth is more complex than the helical rhetoric or the spiral spieling of some public figures. Its roots run deep into the traditions of the bureaucracy. References to the Manual, agency directives, procedural memo-randa, and legal codings are part of it. They must be shared to some extent with the informed public, but not so much that the inner workings of the bureau are revealed.

The bureaucratic writer must remember that the government preserves for long periods of time most of the pieces of paper that it generates for record. Auditors and others bent on pointing fingers periodically invade the files in search of somebody else's mistakes. The key to protective avoidance is the use of words that may be subject to interpretation.

There are several schools of thought as to how to avoid clear communication. Some would argue for brevity on the theory that a short message provides less to criticize. There is something to be said, however, for the other extreme. By writing profusely and redundantly and inconclusively, so much is provided to examine and correlate and decipher that auditors may become discouraged, if not confused. General words are safer than explicit terms which might precipitate precise understandings. The abstract and the passive add seasoning to any communicative offering. Mixing in a few extra phrases and clauses may also improve the flavor. Introduced generously, these ingredients allow each recipient to satisfy his taste.

The helical oratory of politics sometimes borrows simple terms from the bureau's glossary. For instance, New York Governor Hugh Carey, in presenting his "retrenchment" budget for $10.7 billion, promised that it would necessitate no new taxes. As a substitute for taxes he resorted instead to "new income measures" which he estimated would yield $328 million.

Numbers play a big part in the language of bureaucracy, particularly form numbers and Manual section numbers and Agency Directive codes. To illustrate, under a given system wastebaskets might be designated as Schedule 23 equipment, while fire extinguishers might be classified under Schedule 37. In an emergency, employees may avoid using a fire extinguisher to put out flames in a wastebasket due to confusion over schedule numbers and the required administrative processing that applies to each schedule. If Section 79 of the Manual requires that a report be filed each time an extinguisher is used, this may be a deterrent. If it also takes a Form 2380 and a Form 1911 to satisfy requirements of the control agencies, there may not be any quick action. The extinguisher must also be recharged after it is emptied. Anybody familiar with the Manual's language could figure out how to do the related paperwork. But the Manual is large and not always easily understood. There should be no surprise, therefore, when employees put out the fire with water from a flower vase. As an unnumbered piece of equipment, the vase can be recharged at the drinking fountain without filling out any forms.

Field employees are notoriously unschooled in the language of the system. They are a cause of many auditors' ulcers. Surveyors and foresters and construction men do such things as build toilets on mountain tops without proper authorization. Such field workers may not know one government form from another, and unfortunately may not even give a damn. All that they may know is that they have to beat their way through the poison oak without the convenience of ordinary sanitary facilities. Perhaps they can be excused for not wanting to squat in the bushes when they perform their natural functions. They might even be commended for acting on their own initiative. However, there is really no excuse for their failing to file the proper forms for equipment fabrication. One of their most flagrant violations is the use of official forms in lieu of toilet tissue. Prohibition of such practices is spelled out comprehensively in the Manual, but some employees evidently do not understand the terminology.

Knowing the Process

A primary function of the system is to convert volumes of raw input into an optimized flow of output. Communication networks pouring out vast quantities of data contribute to a smoothly operating bureau. Even though substantive data input may be minimal, it can be chopped into pieces and enriched to assure a respectable output. To provide for days when there may not be any input at all, some data can be stockpiled and fed into the mill as needed to sustain a continuous discharge. The health of the bureau depends upon this circulation through its arteries. Although some throttling of the stream may be necessary, this should be limited to important information that might be misused. Items of no real significance can be disseminated profusely without fear. In case of doubt, the valves should be adjusted on the side of plenty. With a high-capacity copier, this is easy.

The literary products of the bureau have a long way to go in the maze. Approvals must be obtained step by step in progression through the management layers, providing insurance against precipitous action and against concentration of responsibility. The sequencing from desk to desk and from basket to basket assures integrated application of the diverse talents in the agency. It fosters an orderly working climate where paper can flow at a

measured pace. Those critics who would shortcut
procedures tend to ignore the time needed to ripen
bureaucratic products. If they had their way, projects would be undertaken with a fervent and head-
long rush. This is certainly no way to run a government. Important papers must be pondered without
disruptive enthusiasm. By deliberate and un-
emotional contemplation of the many variables,
the dangers of overlooking something are
minimized.

A scene something like the following is enacted
routinely in many government agencies:

The bureau maintenance chief called the office
of Agency Contracts Administration.

"Mr. Bogwaddle isn't here," the secretary explained. "I'm afraid I can't help you."

"I'm concerned about expediting the interagency agreement with the Transportation Agency
for joint maintenance of equipment."

"Mr. Bogwaddle has been handling that personally."

"Yes, I know that . . . When will he be back?"

"He's on vacation this month."

"Who is handling it for him?"

"He hasn't given it to anybody. I know the
lawyers have to see it yet. But he was going to talk
to them about it . . ."

"The lawyers have already seen it," he
informed her.

"Yes, but they still have to surname it."

"Why didn't they do that when they had it?"

"They have to see it in its final form, of course."

"Couldn't you call them and have them sign
it?"

"Mr. Bogwaddle will do that."

"How many surnames does it have now?"

The girl shuffled papers. "Your name is on it,

and the Bureau Chief, the Assistant Administrator, the Administrator, the Budget Officer, the Executive Analyst, the Program Analyst, the Chairman of the Interagency Contracts Committee, the Comptroller . . ."

"That ought to be enough."

"The legal staff still has to endorse it."

"It's already been through the same mill at the Transportation Agency, and it will get the same full treatment in the General Services Agency. Three legal reviews, three budgetary reviews, three program reviews, and I don't know how many committees."

"And sometimes the Finance Administrator and the Attorney General have to see these," the girl offered helpfully.

"My God, you've brightened my whole day," he groaned. "Thank you for all your help. Give my regards to Mr. Bogwaddle."

In addition to the regulatory effect of fellow workers, there are other factors which inherently control the work flow in the bureaucracy. The various progress reports and status forms required by the Manual are very helpful in assuring an uninterrupted paper discharge. Typically they are comprehensive in detail and call for tedious conformance with a specified format. If properly prepared they can occupy a large part of the work week, leaving hardly enough time to do the work upon which the report is being made. In some bureaus where the basic workload is light, the reports on activities may be welcome relief from boredom, and also stimulative of the imagination. In fact, some of the most successful members of the hierarchy first won recognition as progress reporters.

When a piece of paper finally comes out the end

of the sinuous pipeline, the recipient can be confident that the programmed relay system has processed it till hell won't have it. Through disinterested stroking, the highest quality of bureaucratic output is assured. Everybody will agree that this requires a finely tuned apparatus and a devoted regiment of operators. That which appears immobile from the outside is the epitome of preservational activism on the inside. There is movement at every angle within the institutional sphere, maintaining a self-contained momentum which keeps the mass moving in a single direction.

Knowing Fellow Bureaucrats

Manualists

The custodians of the Manual lead peaceful lives as long as they are content to massage the pages routinely. However, now and then a manualist recognizes opportunities for extending control over other residents of the bureau. From that moment forward his life becomes more complicated. In trying to exercise control, he will be seen as a threat and will even run the risk of becoming a leader. He is better off to resist such temptations and to spend his time shaping his limited task to make it most comfortable.

Manualists come in many forms. They are often the tentacles of the control agencies, wriggling down the corridors as specialists, coordinators, analysts, or anything else that you might not want if you were paying for it out of your own pocket. They and those who conspire with them are careful not to advertise the leverage which they write into the Manual until they have it in final print. Once a new edict is locked into the Book, the process is practically irreversible. Any protest can be massaged for years if the manualists want it that way.

To illustrate with a case drawn from real experience, there was the chief technician who complained to his bureau chief: "Our system is fouled up because we can't get our instruments calibrated. We used to go directly to the Federal Bureau of Standards but our staff nuisances put a stop to that, you remember. The Manual now dictates that the Central Service Branch administer interagency contracts like that. Maybe they'll eventually get through to the Bureau of Standards, but it seems to take forever."

"What does the CSB add to the process?"

"Several weeks and a lot of overhead cost, and while they're at it they try to figure some way to rob the federals of the calibration work."

"The CSB doesn't know how to calibrate precise instruments."

"No, but if they stall long enough maybe they can get somebody trained to do it."

"That's why they got themselves written into the Manual to handle those contracts. They go through each one to see what they can rake off."

"Too bad we can't get the General Services Agency to investigate the CSB. They would see through the whole mess."

"Yes, it takes one to know one."

The manualist and his symbiotic associates will have special interest in the agency's program control system. Everybody knows that program control is essential to a well-run enterprise. However, in the hands of an accomplished bureaucrat it can be turned into a comforting plan for self-preservation. The system can be designed to assure a great volume of paperwork which confounds many and conceals all but the largest of mistakes. It must give special attention to suggested departures from routine. Through management by exception, those activities which have been going on for years may be allowed to continue while new ideas can be held up until they have been fully examined for potential impact.

An inseparable companion and instrument of the Manual and the program control system is the Agency Directive (A.D.), which has widespread appeal to true bureaucrats and has caused more than a few ulcers among oppressed civil servants in lower levels. Aggressors who would enlarge their advantages will sew themselves into new activities with this needle. They can fabricate an A. D. putting themselves in charge of something and then get one of the collaborating members of the hierarchy to sign it. The perpetuators of the Manual use the A. D. to interpret the law of bureauland exactly the way they want it. The Paperwork Committee, for example, may demand via this instrument that the permission of the committee be obtained before any revisions are made in brochures and guidebooks. The executive who sanctions such expansionary moves will be sure to make the committee accountable to him. He will support these aggressions as long as they promise him control over the whole game. By tying the money and the Agency Directives with his own ribbons he can spread his influence throughout the agency.

The gospel of the Manual must be preached. A heavy burden rests upon the personnel department and other staff units close to the corner office to carry the message. This is accomplished by memoranda and bulletins and an array of training classes. They show the way to the unity of purpose so essential to preservation of the bureau. In some agencies this mission has followed the pattern of saturation bombing. The same uniform training is given to all employees, no matter what their function may be.

Deadwood

Among the types indigenous to the bureaucratic landscape are surplus staff members who either laze in their chairs or prowl the maze in quest of amusement. Frugal in their expenditure of energy, they tend to find their ways onto the many committees fabricated for various purposes, including the storage of deadwood. Their primordial need for security may lead them to embrace the system's absolutes instinctively.

Nearly every agency has its share of these torpid hangers-on, who gain their status by outwaiting supervisors reluctant to brave the bureaucratic tangle of prescribed disciplinary procedures. Looking the other way is easier than facing up to malperformance. If the boss cannot transfer the dud to some other unsuspecting supervisor, he can shove him into a quiet corner or take the more painful route of trying to fire him. The latter is a rare occurrence. The agency may thus become a sanctuary for a collection of nonproducers who sit around sleepily from month to month waiting for their paychecks. Most of them will feel that the government owes it to them for suffering through the boredom.

Some less charitable observers would advocate the establishment of a reject section where all the misfits and incompetents could be isolated so that they would not disturb the productive employees.

This has been tried with only limited success. Branding the goof-offs as worthless bums somehow does not shame them into doing any work.

Since most of these people are permanently embedded, provision must be made for their comfort and self-improvement. This includes handy toilets and reading material. In practically all government offices the distribution of publications is generous, so that even the least inspired employee can be well read. Governmental printed matter is made available in massive doses. Additionally, subscriptions are maintained to popular magazines and newspapers so that civil servants who find time on their hands can make themselves better informed. The constant flow of these opportunities stimulates frequent and lengthy debates, between coffee breaks, on current topics of general interest. The high level of literacy and eloquence thus developed is evident in nearly every meeting. Sometimes the discussions even touch upon the work at hand.

Employees unattracted by management's call to their minds sometimes follow alternative pursuits on their own initiative. Desks are crammed with decks of playing cards, crossword diagrams, and statistics on stocks and bonds. Well-worked and reworked calculations of sick leave, vacation, and retirement benefits are commonplace. The broader interests of the females are evidenced by knitting needles, personal letters, and fashion magazines. There is something for everybody.

Committeemen

People assigned to committees are often there because somebody wanted to get them out from underfoot, or because they themselves were looking for haven from labor, or not infrequently because they saw the committee as a device for personal leverage. Since a committee will have a mixture of these types, it can be useful in satisfying several goals simultaneously.

Although many committees appear to do nothing, this appearance is often superficial and illusory. Actually, nearly all committees do something. For example, they have kept some employees out of the welfare lines. If there is nothing for a man to do, he can always be put on a committee. It is not likely to worsen his condition and it will give his supervisor peace of mind.

Information Brokers

There is a special kind of bureaucrat who is not responsible for grinding out the final product of the bureau, but is heavily involved in many areas of activity. This is the information broker. He circulates freely, learning what he can and sharing only what he must. By pocketing the missing links in the data chain he can prevent certain actions and regulate the rate of progress on others.

One advantage that the controller of information has is that the movement of information is generally a duty assigned to unimportant people. Sometimes the most vital information will come from the very bottom. The collector therefore has to move among the lowest employees in search of what is needed. The raw data that are scooped up must be reworked by processes that are usually unexciting. This drudgery is unattractive to many in the labyrinth. Yet the manipulator who can take his gatherings and mold them imaginatively to suit a given executive need is in a position with high potential.

He will learn quickly that the information that he conveys will be most pleasing to the recipient if it is first dressed in the popular fashion. With fancy print and colorful graphics even the most uninteresting data can be made impressive. While information can be embellished to make it more acceptable, effort should not be made to oversimplify it. An information broker who makes his product fully understandable can run himself out of business. He will be better off to emphasize the complexities so that he will be needed to explain them. That which started as simple logic at the lowest working levels can be fertilized with data from other points of origin and compounded so that it requires interpretation by a specialist. The broker must stay close at hand so that he can respond when the call goes out for an interpreter.

Cooperators

The labyrinth has narrow conduits which allow little judgmental latitude. The penalties for deviant behavior usually outweigh the rewards for exceptional output. With all the incentives aimed at conformance, sensible bureaulings will meet official expectations to the maximum of their abilities. Even when they stray they will wear the mask of obedience.

Acceptable performance limits are demonstrated by the efficiency ratings which are issued periodically. Grades in the middle zone of the scale do not require special written justification. Employees understand the restraints and will tolerate a supervisor who brackets them with the flock, free from the stigma of an outer-fringe appraisal. Continuity of favor is assured by merely avoiding commitment to the left or to the right.

This does not take any conscious effort if the rules and rituals are embraced wholeheartedly.

The institutional member who continuously expresses his devotion to hierarchical principles does his part to maintain placid flows in the paper channels and enjoys therefore the gratitude of his associates and superiors. He will thus establish his image as an opponent of disruption and eventually may be marked for advancement. As he rises and becomes more visible, he must be even more careful to manifest his loathing for trouble. Recognized as an advocate of harmony, he will be asked to participate in more and more activities where his accommodative capacity will be appreciated. By all means he should avoid being drawn into open contest with other loyal cooperators who seek management's favor. If frictions do develop, the more competent combatant will arrange that his opponent surface as the disruptor.

Attorneys

A key worker in the maze is the attorney-at-law. From time to time one critic or another of the legal profession will suggest that steps be taken to curtail the rapid spread of influence of attorneys in government. In fact, lawyers everywhere have been subjected to such attack. Critics ask, for example, what would happen if attorneys went on strike. The suggested answer is that logic and fair play would immediately return to the market place and to government. There is no reason, however, to expect such thinning of the ranks. The legal specialists are not going to leave their posts unguarded even for a moment. And that is just as well, since they are desperately needed as interpreters of the government's message.

Many citizens apparently believe that any problem can be solved by enacting another law. Best evidence of this is the hundreds of thousands of laws and regulations turned out each year by deliberating officials from Hawaii to Maine. All of this has placed heavy demands on the nation's attorneys. Growth of the legal fraternity-sorority has been faster than a fertilized weed. The number of lawyers in the United States is approaching half a million, about twice their population in 1957. Government continues to employ them in large numbers. The Department of Health, Education and Welfare has doubled its legal staff since 1970. Other agencies are striving to match this achievement. They have little choice, since legislation written by lawyers requires implementation by lawyers. The Department of Labor, for instance, administered about forty laws in 1960, while today it polices more than three times that number. The federal government is doing what it can to meet the need. It even created its own Legal Services Corporation and has staffed it with more than three thousand attorneys from coast to coast.

In 1977, Chief Justice Warren E. Burger warned that unless more legal conflicts could be settled out of court the country could be "overrun by hordes of lawyers hungry as locusts." He added, however, that he disagreed with Shakespeare's words, "The first thing we do, let's kill all the lawyers." (King Henry VI, Second Part.) He acknowledged that the legal profession has made great contributions to society, but "As with most experts and specialists, they are splendid servants but terrible masters."

Female Bureaucrats

Women in government were generally disadvantaged until Equal Employment Opportunity (EEO) programs were installed in recent years. Now their status has changed drastically, along with the employment conditions of other groups for whom the government's doors have swung open.

In the Department of the Interior, to give a standard example, each Bureau is now required to provide the following:

1. A full-time EEO Officer who reports directly to the bureau head.
2. A full-time Federal Women's Program Coordinator to serve on the staff of the EEO Officer.
3. A Spanish-Speaking Program Coordinator to assist the Bureau EEO Officer carry out programs to promote equal opportunity for the Spanish-speaking.
4. A full-time EEO Officer for each major field administrative or regional office.
5. A Federal Women's Program Coordinator and a Spanish-Speaking Program Coordinator for each major field administrative or regional office.
6. A Spanish-Speaking Program Coordinator at installations near population concentrations of Spanish-speaking people.
7. EEO Counselors as necessary, throughout the bureau, to be readily accessible to employees.
8. A minimum of four EEO investigators.

To oversee compliance, the department has established a Division of Equal Employment Opportunity. It enforces the public laws, executive orders, Civil Service Commission bulletins, and Personnel Manual instructions designed to protect women and the other underprivileged members of the bureaucracy. EEO offices everywhere are docu-

menting the diligent work of the fighters of prejudice. As a result, women especially are beginning to enjoy the many benefits of the institution.
Despite a few outcries of reverse discrimination,
they are getting treatment to compensate them for
past injustices. In the process, they are learning
what experienced bureaucrats already know—that
advancement is not necessarily assured by merit
alone. They also have to learn the bureaucratic
rules.

Even though they have been denied adequate
financial reward, females in the maze have not
lacked influence. The ladies of bureauland have
their own unwritten rules for governing the office.
The file system is a good example. Its woman
manager will likely regard the file room as a private preserve. The system is sometimes less than
effective. Retrieval of records may demand opti-
mism and patience. As a good housekeeper, the
supervisor may be as concerned about the condition of the cabinets as access to the records. The
typical chief of the files is accustomed to such
criticism. She will have seen upstart critics come
and go over the years and she will be justifiably
proud that her system has survived all their
attacks. Most filing practices are admittedly durable. To protect her territory, the queen of the files
will have written into the Manual during her tenure
all the rules necessary to guarantee that the system
will remain her exclusive province.

Some inventive filing specialists have gone
beyond this to gain authority over acquisition of
file equipment throughout the agency. Ostensibly
this is to keep everybody from wasting money on
cabinets. Its real purpose is to prevent the establishment of competing systems. There are easy
ways to get around this rule. Instead of ordering

cabinets the shrewd civil servant will ask for book shelves or a credenza, or requisition an extra desk and use the drawers for filing. One drawer is as good as another for storing private files, as well as lunches and candy bars.

Those who would question such circumvention of the rules should recognize the futility of untangling a regulation that is deeply imprinted and the lifeblood of some proud keeper of the files. The less courageous will leave the system standing there while they walk around it.

The file room can be a lonely place. The chief cannot be blamed if from time to time she brings in other girls to teach them the system. Some conscientious supervisors have developed full-scale rotation programs for the announced purpose of training girls in handling the files. Perhaps because of loneliness there is often a large turnover rate among these file clerks. Just when one gets trained she may become pregnant and be lost to the agency. Rotating the girls frequently from file station to file station tends to compensate for these losses. However, some bureaucrats have questioned whether this continuous flow of clerks is necessary and whether the nomads stay long enough in any place to be of value. They contend that if the girls could settle down and learn the ropes at a single station they might become more content and there might be fewer pregnancies. There is a paucity of statistical verification of this assumption.

With increasing numbers of women aspiring to higher office, filing chores are certainly not as attractive as they used to be. Various efforts have been made to reverse this trend. File clerks have been offered more money, more authority, and more impressive titles. Much still remains to be done. Some analysts advocate the establishment of a division which would be put in complete charge of all records in the bureau. By upgrading the management of this division to full executive status and assigning it authority over paper handling, many benefits could be developed. Uniformity would be high among these.

Even more powerful than files supervisors are some of the secretaries in the executive suites. People in the shelter of a typical government office will usually acknowledge that they are governed by the secretary of the top man. Few will dispute this fact of life, although the executive himself may think that he is in command. Anyway, he will be comfortable in the role that his secretary assigns to him. The script allows him to enjoy the intoxicating atmosphere of the capital halls and to leave the paper mill to others.

For her part, his secretary will often be too busy directing operations to perform common secretarial duties. She may leave telephoning chores to Girl Number Two, except when a calling personage needs special caressing. She will train the other girls in the art of telephonic insulation, to prevent penetration of the office defenses by callers of lowly station or unpromising intent. One effective technique is to place the call on HOLD and wait for the telephone light to go out.

An efficient secretary in an agency headquarters follows a ritual in putting the office in shape for the day's business. First thing in the morning, she puts her coffeepot on; sets the rubber stamp for the day's date; checks the supply of paper clips; waters the potted plants; lubricates her swivel chair; straightens the certificates on the walls; dusts the autographed photograph of the chief executive; inserts yesterday's addenda into her copy of the Manual; replenishes the supply of hand-out literature for visitors at the reception area, including copies of her supervisor's latest speeches; then combs the daily schedules of other executives to list meetings in which her boss should be involved, invited or not.

A good secretary will take pride in the role that she plays. Through the activities of her boss she can enjoy an influence that may be the envy of the agency's feminine ranks and an irritant to the male masses. They will either respect her or resent her. As long as they pay attention, she may not care how they react.

The secretary or administrative assistant of the top man may be as clever as her boss, and may use her wiles to support his efforts. In her own behalf she will manage to put down deep roots. Although she may be capable of doing all the work in her office by herself, she will persuade the personnel analysts to assign her assistant typists and at least one errand runner. Aside from these underlings she will also exercise unchallenged power over the executive's lieutenants.

Malcontents

Any civil service office will develop complaints about working conditions. Actually the bureaucracy does not impose any harsher circumstances on its employees than it does on the populace at large. Any employee problem will get attention eventually as long as there is compliance with the regulations. For example (a true case in an agency in California), a sick worker who has suffered an attack can have an ambulance just as soon as it is cleared through the building manager, the general services agency, the security police, and the administrative chief. First-aid procedures

for such occasions should be spelled out comprehensively in the Manual. An employee can nearly
always be found who has been trained in mouth-to-
mouth resuscitation and the filing of reports on
accidents.

Many complaints stem from the alleged poor
service at government warehouses. The difficulties of getting a requisition processed through
normal channels encourage searching for shortcut
ways to get supplies and equipment. This may
explain the disappearance of office furnishings of
employees who resign or retire. These tendencies
are not confined to civil servants in the lower
levels. Traditionally most chiefs start making
plans for reallocating space the minute the word
gets out about a pending departure. At such times
there is a tendency to bend the rules. Everybody
wants a better office. It is therapeutic. In fact, some
misguided employees find therapy in beating the
system in any way.

As symbols of the system and of sometimes
oppressive authority, government supervisors are
the targets of numerous complaints. A few civil
servants will not appreciate the need for paying
homage to their superiors. There are telltale signs
of the presence of such people. Towels and tissue
may be scattered around the restrooms. Other clues
are scraped paint in the stairways and witty poems
about the agency's executives written on the walls
with grease pencils and crayons. Some of the more
daring may even ridicule political leaders. These
must be erased right away.

There is a definite trend toward more active
defiance of authority. Some bureau inhabitants will
strew paper all over the place just to get attention.
There have even been reports of urination from

government roof tops. Unfortunately none of the rebels has been apprehended, due to confusion caused by the unexpected downpour onto innocent passersby on the sidewalks below. This has been condemned as unbecoming behavior for public employees. It is certainly not regarded as a proper kind of protest against management. After everything is mopped up, the fact remains that defiance has no rightful place in a bureaucracy. The dissidents will come and go, but only the employees who conform will make a lasting contribution to the general welfare. They are the leaders of the future.

Knowing the Surveillants

A control network must be stitched together tightly to limit the movements of the institution's residents. An ordered behavioral system will suppress the open aggressions in officialdom while maintaining an optimum level of general stress.

The surveillance functions of the control agencies tend to be intricate and expensive. These apparently dispensable agencies survive because they are essential to protection of the flanks of public officials. To serve this need, bureaucracies are created to monitor other bureaucracies. Carried to the ultimate, agencies may be assigned to watch each other. This has not met with complete success simply because mutual surveillance stimulates backscratching. (Each agency gives the other a favorable report.) No matter how they are used, surveillance units are popular with dignitaries at the pinnacle because they offer broad control over the beings in the maze. To maximize this service the surveillants will use every bureaucratic device to extend themselves and their

authority. Their status will grow in direct proportion to the depth of their probings. This is
facilitated if endless reports are demanded of those
being scrutinized. The more reports that they are
obligated to prepare, the less time that they have to
do anything that can be scrutinized. Surveillants
need not be dismayed by such diminishing returns,
since the reports themselves serve adequately as
objects of scrutiny. There is a natural tendency for
surveillance units to demand ever-increasing
volumes of reports even after such reporting
becomes the sole activity of the bureau being examined. If the purpose is to nullify the original
function of the bureau, it works very well.

This profuse reporting of activity may be only
distantly related to the basic needs of an agency.
The records produced may be of no use except for
satisfying those who are doing the inspecting.
Since the judgments rendered by the surveillants
must be drawn largely from the reports themselves, careful attention must be given to satu-
rating their contents with favorable commentary
about the functions of the bureau. This can be
enhanced if the report writer has thoroughly re-
searched what the scrutinizer should hear so that a
favorable impact is registered. Since the ranks of
the monitors are often crowded with skeptics, the
fabricator of bureaucratic reports is well advised to
secure outside opinions to reinforce his presentations. A board of consultants has often been used
successfully for this purpose. This may seem unnec-
essarily expensive but, measured against the vast
resources that most bureaus already devote to
satisfaction of the sentinels, it is usually money
well spent.

When the ultimate is reached and all resources

of the bureau are assigned to responding to surveillance, any incremental demand by the scruti-
nizers must obviously be met by an increase in the
population of the bureau. Considering that several
report writers may be needed to satisfy the appetite
of a single control agent, opportunities for expansion are almost unlimited.

Sometimes control and operating responsibilities are combined in a single agency. One of
these hybrids may be known as the Basic
Services Agency (BSA), an omnipotent governmental control arm that presents itself as the para-
gon of bureaucratic virtue. A typical BSA will not
overlook the slightest opportunity to demonstrate
bureaucentric precepts and to spread its benevolent influence. Among its favorite pastimes is
building space allocation. As result of space sur-
veys, employees of all but appointive rank may be
pressed into smaller cubbyholes, fostering
togetherness and a few distractions. For public
satisfaction the gross rent may be reduced, enough
sometimes to balance the decline in work output.

A common requirement that all copy paper be
ordered in standard quantities from the BSA warehouses may result in a regulated paper usage that
is quite satisfying to the regulators. Another noteworthy consequence may be that requisition and
handling costs will increase, and much time will be
spent in waiting for the BSA clerks to process
orders at their remarkably casual pace. This can
provide valuable benefits. It will help the people
standing in line to get better acquainted, and to
compare ideas on how to circumvent the bottle-
neck by alternative reproduction methods. Efficiency may be impaired somewhat but employee
interaction will be clearly enhanced.

The BSA may also have charge of the warehousing and distribution of forms, which may number in the thousands. The subordinate agencies typically will be limited by decree to maintaining minimum supplies in their own stockrooms and ordering special requisition forms which may be used to obtain forms for other purposes. Excesses are thereby avoided and compilation of form consumption statistics is facilitated.

To illustrate how thoroughly such agencies involve themselves in daily activities, consider a real edict which was distributed to supervisors in all bureaus in one state government:

> It has been reported that some agencies are using envelopes to transmit correspondence through the state messenger service. Your attention is directed to Section 15379 of the State Administrative Manual which specifically prohibits this practice. Only fully justified confidential material is to be sent enclosed. In the interest of economy all unnecessary use of envelopes is to be avoided. Supervisors will be held responsible for such use of supplies.

The most remarkable aspect of this case was that many copies of the directive were mailed in separate envelopes.

Any candid administrator of a BSA will concede that his agency plays an essential role in internal surveillance, on the assumption that government units are naturally going to get into mischief. However, he may contend that the BSA abhors being cast as the Gestapo and is only trying to offer centralized services where such can be provided most economically. The truth is that any energetic BSA administrator will already have established a firm hold as the principal control agent, and will work hard to expand his role as the operator of the government machinery.

In response to the rumblings and grumblings
stirred by his missionary efforts, he may explain
that when a management void exists in any agency
he is obligated to intervene and institute his cura-
tive treatment. This assumes that the surveillant
has expertise to share. In truth, the control agency
may not be very efficient. Some of its costs may be
twice as high as its clients would incur by doing the
work themselves, if they were allowed. But the BSA
is not likely to be opened to the light of public
scrutiny. Its costs are largely obscured as sur-
charges on the budgets of the treated agencies. The
invoices for its imposed services are not to be
challenged. An agency being serviced—like a cow
in the pen with an affectionate bull—has to appreciate that the service is by the control agent
himself.

Though lacking in some routine capabilities,
any worthy BSA must have depth of experience in
system manipulation. It will have scouts deployed
throughout the legislative chambers lobbying for
any measure that will enhance the agency's power.
One of the favorite devices is to have a rider af-
fixed to the budget act requiring that all expenditures of any consequence be cleared by the BSA.
Everybody knows that this will involve delays
while the supreme agency combs transactions in
search of ways to extend its dedicated service.

Knowing the Machinery

Computers

Those who still doubt the value of computers in
government systems may as well relax and enjoy
them. The magnificent device is an established
fixture in any self-respecting agency. Its capacity

for complication and expansion of detail is enough to assure its permanency. The commitment to a computer system is irreversible for all practical purposes. Once the electronic bureauling is plugged in, there's no easy way to unplug it.

The introduction of a new computer system makes all kinds of work for the inhabitants of the bureau. Much of the printed matter which guides the agency, such as the Manual, the files, and the forms, must be converted so that the throbbing mechanisms can digest it. Not everybody is equal to this task. New civil servants will have to be recruited to reinforce the staff so that it can carry the new burdens. Not the least of these is the catching and stacking of the output of a machine which can spew a year's records in five minutes. The staff must be able to handle this even though it rests for the remainder of the year.

There are many reasons for the great amount of management attention that electronic computers receive. The value of the machines to the image of an agency is well known. Less recognized but equally important is the machine impact upon the thought process. A properly programmed computer will give any answers that are desired. Some carpers have charged that this gives refuge from reality. Although a certain amount of such insulation is inevitable, it is not all that bad. If protection from reality is assumed to be a disadvantage, it is outweighed anyhow by the discipline that these benevolent devices impose upon analytical procedures. This precludes leaping to easy and sometimes deviant solutions.

The computer age has brought a higher degree of centralization, which yields many benefits. Centralized machine and programming facilities provide the many merits of standardization and additionally assure that calculations will be in the hands of disinterested workers who are divorced from the problem areas and are therefore unfettered by firsthand knowledge. This tends to minimize any prejudice that would lead to quick conclusions.

By placing data processors in a central location insulated from the work scene, more machine capacity can be utilized. This enhances the feasibility of larger computers. An alternative arrangement would place smaller machines at the production site. Although such equipment might be less expensive, even in the aggregate, it would not always be fully employed and would not allow the greatest development of potential for the organization as a whole. Since all of these sophisticated tools are expensive, they must be used as much as possible. Idle time must be avoided at all cost.

Control agencies have not been entirely successful in persuading other bureaus of the wisdom of a shift to centralized computing services under the management of the control agencies. They have complained that the orientation of the operating units is toward ownership of their own machines, disregarding the obvious benefits of central large-capacity facilities. There has been some feeling that the federal government is partly responsible for this resistance in lower levels of government, since some federal agencies granting funds to state and local units reportedly prefer computers dedicated to the subsidized program.

The incentive to gain control of the computer is easily understandable. Its commander enjoys status just because he is entrusted with one of the most expensive playthings in the labyrinth. Those bureaucratic leaders who approved installation of the equipment will automatically be supporters of its custodian. His position is further enhanced by his knowledge of what has entered and is stored within the vitals of the magnificent device.

Computers are among the fastest devices ever invented. They can therefore spray mistakes all over the maze and challenge common civil servants to find them. In fact, a computer is a kind of magnifier. Both the good and the bad in a bureau will be amplified once the magnetic memory devices are actuated.

Government reports are increasingly dependent upon computer output and therefore tend to take longer to produce. This is particularly true if the report deals with advanced subject matter which must be programmed. The employee responsible for the programming will know the computer language backwards but will have to be trained to understand the report. This need for translation from people language to machine language and vice versa is why a report which used to take a month to turn out by hand processing is now delivered in twelve months through the automatic system.

In the most sophisticated agencies the computer is now entrusted with the keeping of files and with information retrieval. Anybody who wants something that used to be filed in a cardboard folder in a steel cabinet must now send his request to the computer unit and wait for the printout. The lines waiting for this service tend to grow longer. This is not necessarily because the devices are popular. Sometimes it's because the data stored in the electronic entrails are being updated. This takes time. New entries must be checked and this can only be done by a specialist in computer technology, who knows which way the wheels turn even without understanding the subject matter being processed. The information eventually delivered may sometimes be puzzling, possibly due to its long confinement within the sterile cabinetry.

Despite its retarding effect upon some kinds of bureaucratic processes, the computer is popular with bureaulings who want assignments insulated from executive interference. The proprietary language of the computer room and the mysteries of the equipment itself assure that members of the bureaucratic hierarchy will seldom enter, except to introduce visiting dignitaries for special tours of the electronic protectorate. The employees in the computer room would be endangered if anybody outside their insulated walls could understand what they were doing. The confusion that they generate is their best protection. Since government agencies are not usually guided by the profit motive, some of their people tend to be fascinated by computer complexities without worrying about economic justification.

The defenders of the computer concede that during World War II a computerized supply system did provide thirty thousand footlockers to a military unit that needed only thirty, and that a fourteen-man unit at an isolated station received thirty carloads of peas due to a similar electronic error. However, they argue that the computer should not be blamed. And they may be right. The machines are innocuous enough until they are brought together with fuzzy-minded management. After the mid-1940s computers came into the hands of many people who did not understand them, due to the persuasiveness of the wide-ranging salesmen from the computer industry. They found plenty of willing buyers in the various units of government. Suspecting that there might be a problem, the Bureau of the Budget issued a regulation in 1961 calling for full justification of the installation of a computer by any government agency. However, these approvals turned out to be easy to obtain. In some cases, even where new programs were not being introduced, the numbers of computers and computer personnel continued to expand rapidly.

With between seven and eight thousand computers employed in processing the Government's business transactions alone, and with more than one hundred different payroll systems covering the Government's employees, it is probably too late to ask whether the Government should be in the computer business at all. Such questions have been raised.

Copiers

In most government offices, the xerocopier has become almost as common as the pencil sharpener. While access to the equipment is freer in some agencies than in others, practically nobody is denied the opportunity to share in the benefits.

In buildings housing competitive units, or where the purpose of one unit is to keep the other under surveillance, some limits necessarily are placed upon access to copying facilities. Otherwise, privileged information could fall into the wrong hands. In such cases, the simple answer is to equip each section with its very own machine. When this has been done, invariably copying volume has increased to full capacity on each side of the barrier. This favorable result is practically always accompanied by the additional benefit of wider employment of file clerks and paper warehousemen.

Capacity can be maximized by installing the fastest machines. Ideally, they should be located close to the largest groups of employees and obscured from executive scrutiny. Users will feel less inhibited if they can copy in privacy. This causes little disadvantage to management since the executive suite will have its own reproduction equipment anyway. To help in attracting the mass of users, a high quality of paper should be supplied. Coin-operated copiers for personal business should be outlawed from government buildings. They are insulting and damaging to morale.

Recognizing Status

Like any animal habitat, the labyrinth has its system of rating the status of those who reside therein. Those who wish to live at peace will accept their rankings without complaint and will respect the status of others. This is a fundamental of bureaucracy and must be embraced without question.

The location of an office is a well-known indicator of the status of its occupant. Any bureaucrat with a corner office has come a long way. He will have nearly arrived if the corner is on a floor of the building where he can rub elbows with the elite. A keen observer may note subtle differences in the lighting from office to office in the bureaucratic row. The executive who has real status is likely to have his drapes drawn at least partially. There may be a floor lamp and table lamps in the room, controlled by dimmer switches. His subordinates will get by with ceiling fixtures which brighten their rooms from wall to wall. They understand what these differing circumstances signify. Darker rooms are for executive pondering, while light rooms are for delineation of minor details.

Much time is devoted to drawing organization charts. Some agencies have special staff groups for this. As a device for recognition, the chart is a strong satisfier. It can take various forms. Most have rectangular boxes connected by straight lines. The largest box is usually at the top. It sometimes has a double frame. Certain impressive labels are inserted in the boxes. Thickness of lines and the space between rectangles may be used to depict degrees of status. Broken lines sometimes indicate level of interference. Infrequently circles or ellipses are drawn instead of rectangles. The boxes are nearly always arranged in tiers. The lowest row is still a long way from oblivion.

Getting Ahead

One of the less effective incentives in the government service is salary. Standardization of pay scales assures that nobody in a given bracket will be singled out for special reward for his accomplishments, no matter how outstanding they may be. This is the democratic way. It effectively discourages those who would show off their talents to the dismay of their associates.

An aspiring bureaucrat therefore may concentrate less on hard work and more on establishing friendly relationships with the boss. At the supervisor-subordinate interface, the opportunities for backscratching are seemingly infinite. The employee who is willing to go out of his way to accommodate his superior can find comfort under an umbrella of gratitude. His offerings can come from whatever he has in surplus, but words of praise are especially welcomed by the head man. A proficient scratcher will average approximately one salute and one plaudit per office hour, making sure that each of these registers well on the supervisor.

Chapter 4

the Middle-Echelon Bureaucrat

A bureaucrat who has climbed onto a middle berm of the pyramid has already absorbed a liberal education in the rules, the language, the procedures, and the apparatus of the system. He will know the tenants of the lower tiers, who have been his associates or competitors. However, as he enters the executive environment he will see those underlings in a different light. He will have to find some way to make them respond to his new status. At the same time he will have to learn how to deal with peers, to caress the hierarchy, to get budget approvals, to protect territory, to expand territory, and to survive. As a first lesson, he should study the habits of his new neighbors.

The Home Base

The bureau's leaders display the most courage

when they are operating within their own territory. Outside those boundaries they may feel less
sure of themselves. Within the security of his office the bureaucrat will be comforted by maintaining symbols of that security such as special furnishings, hard-bound copies of the Manual, and a
brass nameplate. To establish a defense perimeter,
the furniture can be arranged so that obstacles
stand across a direct path from the door. By orient-
ing the desk away from the window, the executive
in residence assures that his guests will have to
squint at the glare when they face him across it.

Whatever is visible on the desk should be prepared for examination. A desk calendar, for example, is partly for display. While it may list meetings of some importance, it must also be covered
with notations which are hard to decipher and
which in fact may mean nothing at all. An executive cannot appear important unless his calendar is
crammed with entries. He and his secretary must
be able to understand it but his visitors must see
only that it is full.

The area assigned to a receptionist or secretary should be located so that interception of visitors is facilitated. The executive whose office is at
the end of a long corridor and whose secretary is located so that she can monitor the approach enjoys a
safe space allocation.

Bureaucrats like to insulate themselves by
placing their subordinates in rows of offices radiating out from the chief's corner. The depth of the
insulation depends on how far down the corridors
space can be claimed for the aggressor's territory.
With an ambitious bureaucrat in each of the four
corners of the building, there may be no shortage of
excitement for the subordinates who hang their coffee cups in the offices near the center.

Meetings

Meetings are part of the bureaucratic tradition. While they may have a well-established format and seating arrangement, not many of these get-togethers are memorable. They are not expected to be. Their main purpose is to occupy the calendar on a given day at a given time. Those bureaucrats who want to establish or maintain or expand their status will follow the tradition of holding regular meetings. The authority to command the presence of others must always be used to fullest advantage.

A typical conference table is usually designed to accommodate a limited number of top executives. The rest of the room may be occupied by rows of chairs so that the lower staff can observe the leadership at work. The only rub is that as the years go by and reorganization is piled upon reorganization nobody may be absolutely sure any more of the exact order of rank. There may be chairs at the table to invite those adventurous enough to intrude. Gradually the more aggressive subordinates may move up to the table. When this occurs, certain of the more independent chieftains are likely to drift into the audience section, confusing the distribution of authority in the room. Unless this is kept under control, the boss will find himself surrounded by eager underlings while he converses afar with his top lieutenants who have taken refuge in the rear rows.

While routine meetings are seldom important, a special conference may have all kinds of potential. In preparing for such an event, therefore, the bureaucratic host should assign responsibility for the details to subordinates and collaborators, making sure that assignments are duplicated fully and that everybody is accountable to him. For extra insurance somebody should be designated as the coordinator. But his authority should be minimized and all important decisions must be reserved for the leader, who can issue instructions directly to any of the workers without informing the coordinator. This will provide a maximum of flexibility. It will also keep the coordinator properly nervous as he scrambles to find out what the leader has said and done.

The host may extend personal invitations to those in the highest levels, even if he knows that some of them will decline. They will be pleased to be remembered, and some of them will even enjoy declining. Therapeutic advantages therefore accrue to both the inviter and the invited.

A true bureaucrat is likely to be at ease in meetings of any kind. He will be stimulated by the urge to impress those who surround him. While he strives to stand out in the crowd, his neck will never stick out as far as his tongue. He will be flexible even to the extent of agreeing with both sides of an argument if it serves his purpose.

To gain the upper hand in a long meeting a prudent bureaucrat may abstain from taking liquids for several hours preceding and will visit the restroom immediately before entering the conference room. By arriving with an empty bladder he will be prepared to overcome those who suffer increasing hydrostatic pressures as the meeting wears on.

Committees

A committee can be an especially comforting expedient to cope with difficult decisions. With carefully defined instructions the group can ponder a critical decision interminably. Nobody can blame an executive who wants an important proposal thoroughly examined by a committee before facing the consequences of action.

A bureaucrat must scramble to take care of himself when committees are being formed. He always has to remember to be cooperative, to raise his hand at the first call to duty. Other volunteers will line up quickly to protect their flanks. If the first volunteer has done his homework properly, he will have arranged for one of these to nominate him as chairman. Upon his selection by the appointing power he must remember to protest modestly, knowing that the way to cinch the assignment is to appear slightly reluctant. While he waves his hand in a limp gesture of acquiescence, the chairman will count the favors he owes those who have elected him to the choice spot. He will take care of them, and they know it.

The committee is used sometimes to prolong a position of advantage. Some bureaus owe much to this tool. The wise manager will get his followers named to committees which influence agency policy and he will work to keep these committees in existence beyond their normal lives. This can be accomplished through the reporting process. The reports of the committee can be labeled as interim documents and can include recommendations for certain adjustments in the system. The committee will give itself the job of monitoring and evaluating the modifications and thereby ensure a long-range assignment.

To guarantee that a minimum of delegation of authority passes down to lower levels, a shrewd bureaucrat will often call for a committee circumventing the usual organization channels. It is a good way to get around subordinates who have independent tendencies. In such cases, however, extreme caution must be exercised in selecting the chairman of the group. The person chosen for this role must be fully willing to undermine his associates. There is an ever present danger of collusion between the committeeman and the subordinate being bypassed. Backscratching between subordinates can lead to a bureaucratic knee to the groin which is particularly painful.

Backscratching is essential in important areas such as establishing policy on the format of project billboards. The usual way to accomplish this is to appoint a committee and to charge it with improving the public image of the agency through proper identification of project facilities. Any group embarking upon such a vital mission must understand that its real purpose is to parcel out the agency's glory among its executives. Every member of the high command wants his name on the billboards. Ideally everybody would have his name next to the administrator's in big letters. Each member of the committee will have interests to serve that must be reconciled with others through compromise, One executive will insist that his name be most prominent on the signs nearest the main highways. Another will be most interested in those at tourist centers. Some bureaucrats are especially finicky about the format of commemorative plaques. Such differing desires provide opportunity for the necessary compromise.

Those critics who condemn committees as costly and ineffectual overlook the more subtle benefits offered inherently by group massage. General morale can be enhanced by getting committee endorsement of a policy that management has already adopted but not yet announced. A decree so blessed will gain wider acceptance through democratic participation in its fabrication. The stamp of the group is equally useful in demolishing an idea that generates stomach gas in the executive chambers.

Managers who fear committees should learn the ways to furnish them with constructive guidance. To assure the absorption of knowledge, the group members preferably should not be too well informed initially on the subject matter. They should be selected carefully with this in mind. In their enthusiasm for learning, they can be expected to explore some fruitless tangents. Even though much of the result may defy appraisal, the committee's processing of the data may open worthwhile insights for others. From time to time a conclusion may be reached but the impact is unlikely to be severe. After all, a properly constituted committee will be bound together by a common desire for social acceptance. They will all want to harmonize on a compromise that will not be offensive.

Since the burdens of a committees tend to grow, there are plausible arguments for making them large and creating plenty of subcommittees. Managing the intertwined groups can be demanding. Staff should be assigned to route the mail among the members and to provide them with a steady flow of input data. Meetings should be held frequently. To promote the free exchange of ideas, one committee can be made advisory to another, and vice versa. To integrate the total benefit a special committee can be appointed to study, interpret, and explain the efforts of other committees.

Paperwork

Nothing is much more disquieting for a bureaucrat than being insulated from the information that he needs. This is a situation which he cannot long endure. Something must be done without delay to generate data flow. This is why there is such widespread agreement on the need for continuous operation of the paper processing machines — the typewriters, the xerocopiers, the computers, and the mail carts.

Reports on the progress of activities must be demanded at regular intervals even if progress has not been made. This routine is essential to discipline those who are responsible for progress. One of the primary purposes of bureaucratic reports is to provide the hierarchy with leverage to maintain its status. The requirement of filing of reports helps to remind subordinates of the power incumbent at higher level, or to remind the lower echelons of its absence in their proximity. The substance of reports is usually less important than the fact that they are required to be submitted. The proper level of regimentation is assured when the inflow at the top of the pyramid reaches the point of saturation. Only then can the bureaucratic leadership be confident that the masses are properly oriented. Of course, nobody reads all the stuff that is dumped at the upper end of the tube. Even the writers of the reports know that. What keeps them unnerved, however, is the possibility that eventually something which they write will get attention. The upward flow of paper, therefore, must be prepared in full compliance with all the rules.

In most agencies an uncluttered desk is not a stigma, but empty mail baskets are quite another thing. The flow of paper through an office is an inescapable measure of the importance of the occupant. When the flow dwindles, questions may be raised. To avoid the discomfort of intensified scrutiny, the bureaucrat whose correspondents are neglecting him should generate numerous memoranda and letters on any convenient topics so that early responses will be forthcoming. By keeping paper flying in the channels, attention of management can be drawn in safe directions. The flow can be maintained by a kind of chain-letter process, starting with the lowest echelons. By encouraging staff to generate input into the communication channels and requiring each supervisor to process and add to the material in his in-basket, the compounding of paperwork is guaranteed.

A wise executive will collaborate with the Management Analysis Office and the other paperwork specialists, who are master work fabricators in their own right. Together they must see that the many documents and forms and reports which flow through in quintuplicate are shunted into channels to assure the most exhaustive treatment possible. Other offices may have to expand to cope with the paper stream. This in turn will enhance opportunities for the specialists to peddle their services and to extend their influence. There will be stimulus and enrichment for everybody.

Process enlargement and prolongation are imperative in view of the consequences of oversights. Even the simplest grist for the mill can have deceptive implications. Therefore, seemingly trivial items must get the same treatment as issues of substance.

In those exceptional cases where further paper shuffling would indeed be objectionable, there are ways to bring it to an end. The assignment can be given to the employee who holds the record for the longest report ever written in the agency. By the time a reader finishes one of these treatises he will

have forgotten the subject. Most bureaucratic chieftains hate to wander through such long reports and
will therefore tend to be prejudiced against the subject matter. If this does not squeeze the life out of
the project, more wicked devices may have to be
employed, such as having it proposed aggressively by somebody whom the administrator
loathes.

Any top management may regard bad news as
distasteful and may tend to condemn its carrier.
The aspiring bureaucrat therefore will avoid being
trapped into such a role. He will not touch adverse
reports, shunting them to other desks and other offices whenever possible. If the offensive document
is dropped into his lap and he cannot get rid of it, he
can remold it into a more attractive shape and reduce it to its more favorable elements. Even then he
will attribute the message to other sources and see
that supplementary reports flow through other
channels. Avoidance of knowledge of adversities is
essential if the bureaucrat is to preserve a bright
image. In fact, maintenance of a low profile is always prudent unless the rewards of being conspicuous heavily outbalance the risk.

In any case, those who generate paper for the
mill should avoid irreversible commitment. Even
an implied leaning toward a definitive position
may come back some day to haunt. Ideally perhaps nothing would be said at all. However, in the
bureaucracy everybody is expected to contribute to
wordage. With this as a rule, probably the best
strategy is to devote most of the disgorging to de-
scribing the given problem and commenting on the
efforts of others to solve it. In this way, the subject
will get attention and the writer can display his
knowledge of it while withholding his own sug-

gestions for action. If he is proficient in these literary meanderings, his offering will be accepted as a conscientious attempt to be involved.

To keep the overseers satisfied, everything must be converted into ritual. Paperwork must be standardized, and performers in the rites must be programmed for stock response. If all goes well, the many shafts and gears will turn like clockwork and very little noise will drift into the executive chambers to incite inquiry. Instead, a soothing flow of paper will attest to progress and self-sufficiency.

One of the most important functions of executives and semiexecutives is signing papers — memoranda, letters, forms, and contracts. A man who signs hundreds of times in a month can develop peculiar dexterity with the pen, a talent that may become widely recognized and even saluted. The size of the signature, the weight of pen, and the boldness of stroke are factors that separate leaders from followers. A symbol of distinction is a signature which cannot be read literally. Only a lowly bureaucrat, one suffering from deficient ego, would sign so that his name was legible. As a rule of thumb, a twelve-letter name should not be signed so that more than four letters can be clearly identified.

Bold artistry as a signer should be coupled with a high volume of output. The more signatures per day, the more impact on bureaudom. Fortunately an overseer is not expected to understand everything that he signs. If he stopped to read all that stuff, he would just clog the communication channels.

Some of the best bureaucratic training is in ghostwriting for the hierarchy. The chief execu-

tive seldom writes his own letters. This is dele-
gated down through the sieves in the system to
somebody who is a specialist in writing communications for somebody else. This professional writer
knows that the message he concocts must be directed to those who review his work rather than to the
ultimate recipient. The standard response must enhance the image of the agency, sidestep controversy, and flow in words that are soothing to the
chain of reviewers. It should be vague, friendly,
and hopeful, and appreciative of the inquiry which
called for the response.

In the seasoning that he undergoes as the years
go by, the bureaucrat learns that even though paper flow is a kind of lifeblood for the system the
printed words on the paper do not necessarily convey anything that is particularly useful. This is
equally true of oral deliveries that are made in
committees and staff meetings and general assem-
blies. Of course, very little knowledge is imparted
in the many speeches that bureaucrats deliver at
the slightest invitation. Still, the surgings of paper
and the oral disgorgings represent about all that
the bureau has to serve its need for communication. In gauging the flood, much must be left to interpretation. Most attempts to decipher the verbal
vomitings tend to lead to increased confusion. Any
bureaucracy can thrive on a certain measure of
this.

Coping with Subordinates

In bureaudom the overseer role may be played
in ways that are traditional everywhere, but it also
has twists peculiar to government. Familiarity
with the knots in the red tape separates the professional from the novice. Ignorance of the Manual's

intricacies would place the overseer at the mercy of helpers who could destroy him. The bureaucratic tangle is an ideal hiding place for malperformance. Finding out how something gets done is hard enough, but analyzing mistakes may be nearly impossible if the perpetrator knows how to use the system for refuge.

To ensure orderly interfaces, the limits of authority must be drawn sharply. Nondelegators and delegators alike can take pride in showing the literary pieces that serve this purpose. In the hegemonic arena, where documents in general are a source of much delight, the delegation orders are on display for all to see — while the authors may regularly bypass channels, waving pleasantly as they go by. Less puzzlement might be generated by the nondelegator who would openly advertise his intentions to be a dictator.

Delegation of authority may be a common subject of discussion at the agency conference table. In fact, in some organizations the executives talk about it often. They spend a lot of time in defining the authority of their subordinates. The files are choked with delegation orders. Although a flood of paper flows through their offices each day, they do not see this as a sign of their reluctance to share command. They view delegation as unworkable unless the subordinates are willing to carry the load. They reason that the greater responsibilities must be shouldered at top level. Leaders themselves must give attention to such all-important items as vacation schedules, convention attendance, format of reports, and the wording of agency billboards.

Motivation

The level of competence in a bureau is difficult to raise. There has been ample demonstration that enlargement of the staff will not do it. Sophisticated management systems and devices may give the illusion of competence but a critical examination of the net output is unlikely to show an improvement. Supportive mechanisms such as the computer and the copier can grind away all day and accomplish little except multiplication of the flaws in their input data.

Some aggressive supervisors are unable to understand why their demands yield such diluted response. Although they may penalize the laggards for resistance to executive goading, they should realize that the system really offers little opportunity to put a recalcitrant down. A reading of the Manual might suggest that the performance rating rules could be used to force the troops into line. But the tradition of avoiding high or low grades on the report card leaves little room for coercion.

The avoidance of distinctions in performance ratings has been further encouraged by the trend toward full disclosure of information. Many personnel departments have responded to this pressure by requiring that all appraisals in civil service examinations, and the identification of the rater, be made available to the employee being rated. A supervisor who might otherwise have been candid about his subordinate's deficiencies will give him a passing grade and may even praise him, for the record and for the maintenance of peaceful relationships.

Some bureaucrats use comparative statistics to motivate their paper handlers. They keep staffs busy compiling records of the flow through the mill. To be fair in setting the standards of performance, credit should be given not only for the number of reports but also for the page length of each.

An employee with an aversion for brevity can therefore still be competitive, if he wants to be.

Each employee in the bureau should be encouraged to feel that he participates in management. This can be accomplished by comprehensive definition of agency objectives. For each one of the listed goals, subordinate units can be required to present their plans for implementation. This will include the development of more limited aims for each unit which can be integrated to achieve the broader objectives. Design of the necessary forms and other documents should be assigned to specialists who understand and subscribe to the essential complexities.

By inviting this broad-scale participation, top management has every right to expect that attitudes in the lower echelons will be reshaped and will become more responsive to command. To be sure that participative subordination is achieved, the administrator should insist that reports on goals come up the line regularly. Those who would otherwise withhold commitment are therefore at least obligated to put something on paper. They should be discomforted also at intervals by staff review of compliance.

Most bureaus are dedicated to participative mulling of information. If by some chance constructive action ensues, having shared discussion so generously the commanding executive is entitled to take the credit. The resentment of the masses will not be unmanageable. On the other hand, if the product of deliberation is judged to be a failure the contributors at all levels can join together to present a low profile.

The illusion of activity may be more important than activity itself. A supervisor inspecting a place where work is assumed to be in progress can be deceived by displays of paper or by energetic people or by ringing telephones. Employees of minimal talent will learn to erect this facade quickly whenever inspection is imminent. Although a manager may have little patience with such deception, he must recognize that in approaching the lethargics he has to avoid any action that can be labeled as punitive. If an employee has demonstrated that he is completely unable to work and there is no place to hide him, the great labor of compiling the encyclopedia of data for a disciplinary hearing has to begin. And in the end, likely as not, the boss will be painted with the black hat, as a tyrant incapable of understanding the sensitivities of the lard-bottom.

Wheel Spinners

A special problem is presented by the willing but unproductive worker who expends his energies in deepening his anchorage. Many of these have stagnated in the middle of the supervisory ranks. Often their difficulties are compounded by their reluctance to hire subordinates who might threaten the supervisor's job. The work will pile up while the boss struggles painfully to rationalize his lack of progress. Over his lengthy career he will have compiled a list of scapegoats who can be accused of throwing roadblocks in the way. His favorite is likely to be the Basic Services Agency. Just about anybody will accept a story with the BSA cast in the role of obstructionist. The typical stagnated supervisor will have suffered loudly through a long series of unyielding regimes. The system itself is his complete villain. He will tell anybody about it. But few listeners will want to hear his defensive complaints any more.

The conscientious incompetent will often meditate on his own predicament. Pressed by workload and impatient supervisors, he may attempt to shift his course. The thought of sharing his responsibilities with others may upset him. In fact, it may make him nauseous. But he can expect that the hierarchy may parcel out his undone work to other sections. As soon as they learn the ropes they may absorb his whole function. If he accepted one or more of the ambitious subordinates whom management would thrust upon him, the competition for his own job would become unbearable. Every one of the top candidates has to be suspected. Especially strong defenses have to be thrown up against the brilliant and well-liked aspirant who works like a slave. This kind is a genuine menace.

The best bet for a besieged supervisor is to bring in several of the lesser applicants and to spread the work thinly among them so that the impact of their entry will be diluted. Extreme care must be exercised in making assignments to the recruits to ensure that each learns only a limited part of the job. Keeping an eye on all the new helpers will leave the incompetent more burdened than before, but at least it may get the overseers off his back.

Followers

The bureaucrat who needs insulation can surround himself with uninspired conformists who will obey if not respect him. This enables him to float rather comfortably in mediocrity. It allows him to have his own way and to suppress the ambitious upstarts who come along from time to time. By giving first priority to his own security from bureaucratic onslaught, he will be able to make decisions unhampered by the ideas of others. The real yes-men will assure him of that.

Yes-men are ready subjects by definition and will behave without being pushed. In contrast, some lieutenants of a different stamp will inherently need their own identity and may even feel entitled to their own opinions. Although some of these may possess outstanding qualifications, they should be kept under constant surveillance to assure that they do not gain dangerous prominence in the organization. The intelligent subordinate who wants to stand and be judged on his own talents may have reasonably honorable intentions. But this does not matter. In striving for his own identity he represents a threat to the incumbent management. As his abilities become recognized he may gain a following which, though unofficial, may tend to dilute the authority of the appointed leader. This cannot be tolerated.

Such talented underlings must be governed sternly. The opinions which they volunteer must be rejected or usurped. In either case the object is to enhance the stature of the leader while keeping the subordinate in his place. When the rejected advice turns out to be right, the employee should be penalized for not following through on his convictions. If the ideas borrowed from him pay off, he will be expected to join the others in cheering the leader for his courage in bringing them to fruition. This is the minimum required by good taste.

In drawing a circle of followers care must be exercised that the group profile is everywhere lower than that of the leader. Just one tall subordinate can spoil the picture. If he cannot walk in a crouch when so ordered, he should be erased from the circle. This does not mean that close followers should be small in stature. They must only look that way.

Lady Lieutenants

Any executive with a lady lieutenant may be confronted one day by a nervous subordinate presenting a complaint against the female tyrant. The wording of the protest will vary from office to office but invariably it will be made in the interest of agency image and efficiency. The chief will be assured that all of the people respect him personally but regard his assistant as something of a dictator who tends to shove others around. She will be accused of using his name as a weapon anytime she meets the slightest resistance. She will be blamed for the resignation of employees who could not stand her.

When confronted with such charges, the chief can thank his informant and express his concern. However, he should point out the great competence of his lieutenant, the extent of her tenure, and her acquaintanceship with important people throughout the government structure. If more action is needed, he should make a resolution to do something about the problem sometime. But he must not be hasty.

The bureau's leaders know that they must be especially patient and tender with women subordinates. This is a tradition which still endures. However, regardless of sex and related sensitivities, all employees must respect the dignity of the government office. Among other things, this means avoidance of attire which may be controversial. Agency leaders must see that policies on proper dress of civil servants are observed. To avoid embarrassment of the administration, women particularly must be encouraged to clothe themselves discreetly. All supervisors should be held responsible for assuring that their subordinates are dressed in a manner that will reflect favorably on the image of the agency. The management will thus demonstrate its determination to deal forthrightly with important problems, protecting the public from offense and sheltering the men of the agency from exposure of female skin.

That executives at high levels do care about such personal matters is shown by the real memorandum below:

M E M O R A N D U M   DATE: June 11, 1975

TO: DEPARTMENT DIRECTORS AND
        BOARD EXECUTIVE OFFICERS
SUBJECT: Coats and Neckties

FROM: Office of the Secretary

> Equality cuts both ways and I think it is quite unfair to require men to wear jackets and ties, and not require women to wear the same. Therefore, I hope that the men in your organization will be told that they don't have to wear coats and ties.
>
> There are certain occasions, such as hearings, court appearances, or other public presentations when more formal dress is appropriate, but those occasions should be obvious to all concerned.
>
> Secretary

Although such involvement at the policy-making level would appear reasonable, some employee reactions have been severe. Previously demure ladies have discarded underthings in tearful protest against invasion of their private rights. Admittedly no policy can be regarded as fully successful if it results in women going around with bare buttocks.

Female bureaulings deserve to be given more opportunity for advancement. Despite their sensitivities about mode of dress, they have adequately demonstrated their ability to conform. There is no better credential for full institutional membership.

Protesters

One of the symptoms of agency illness is the breaking down of the discipline of the masses. This is growing more common. Employee associations are taking more militant stands. A tour of government restrooms will provide insight into the changing mental condition of the civil servant. Demands are being made for softer toilet tissue. Restrooms are getting more crowded. Some employees will sit in there for an hour or more, reading the newspapers or doing crossword puzzles. Of course, some of the more inactive can be excused if their bowels do not move as fast as they used to.

The signs of disinterest and disdain for management run the full range. Aside from the considerable time spent on the toilets, much productive energy is put into tearing towels from the racks, smearing the walls with crayon, and scattering debris on the floor. One of the most common complaints is directed to the poor marksmanship of those who stand at the urinals. The slippery floors in the restrooms have been particularly worrisome to departmental safety engineers.

To give proper attention to these problems the administrative overseers should have a survey made of the use of restrooms. Records should be kept of who goes in and who comes out and how long they stay. Some of the remedial measures which have been considered are reducing the number of toilet stalls and putting in coin-operated locks. These have not been entirely successful. One suggestion which may have merit is to reduce the length and frequency of coffee breaks to control the excessive consumption of liquids and the consequent intensification of traffic at the urinals.

The use of restrooms as headquarters for protest is of growing concern to government leadership. Some of the poetry on toilet chamber walls has been especially insulting to certain overseers, and there is no easy way to stop it. New passages are inscribed as fast as the old are removed. Janitors have scrubbed walls down to the plaster. Where more durable wall paints have been proposed, the Manual's restrictions on building modifications have hindered action. They do not facilitate changing the walls, let alone the number of stools or urinals. But something must be done. Restroom activities in some agencies have risen to crisis proportions. Toilet management will have to get more overseer attention.

Dissidents will remain so under nearly any regime. Since it is their nature to grumble, a change in management will not likely convert them. If they complain without effect, they should be left alone. If they tend toward mutiny, they should be separated from their audience.

Subversives

A more serious hazard is the fellow bureaucrat

who specializes in undermining his associates. The executive who has one of these as a subordinate must be vigilant. Since a subversive lieutenant's plans may not always be clear, his performance should be watched to detect any move which may be threatening. An especially disturbing habit of some subversives is to bring the deficiencies of the boss to the attention of his superiors. For protection, the latter should be informed of this propensity for throat cutting. Dealing with hatchet carriers is unavoidable in the bureaucracy. Having to live with them, the shrewd leader will enlist them on his team and arrange to turn their hatchets outward against the competition.

Nomads

Another kind to watch is the nomadic pest who travels everywhere that he can at government expense, butting into activities without being invited. A typical wanderer may be a flunky whose supervisor regards him to be worthless except as a part-time spy. Nobody wants him around so he is allowed to run loose. Those who would consider releasing him from government service would be well advised to examine his record. Typically he will have seniority coming out of his ears, so that he could never be discharged. If he is declared officially surplus he will bump some good employee who is really needed. The best thing to do is ignore him and let him wander. He is usually harmless as long as he is kept on the road.

Peddlers

There are those frivolously twisted personalities in the bureau who delight in the generation and dissemination of rumors of nearly any kind. Since they create excitement in an environment which sometimes needs it, these bureaulings cannot be dismissed lightly. They are even useful at times for stirring up quiescent recesses in the labyrinth. In the peddling of such bureaucratic tidbits, however, certain rules must be observed. The rumor should have some purpose other than the amusement of the perpetrator and his collaborators. It should be designed to disturb somebody who needs to be disturbed, or to encourage somebody who needs encouragement. Also, its authorship should be concealed. A rumor cannot remain a rumor if its origin can be traced.

Although the peddler may not turn out much work, his inability to keep a secret may be a valuable attribute. While he has to be excluded from certain meetings to keep him from leaking restricted information, there are other times when he can serve as an unofficial conveyor of the news. Confidences that need to be disseminated can be shared generously with him to assure maximum distribution of the word. The extreme importance of the secret must be made clear to him.

Scramblers

Some employees use the government office as headquarters for private enterprises. The rent and the services are free and there may be plenty of time for the extra work. If such activity becomes conspicuous, some managerial attention may be required. For example, a supervisor may feel that too much xerocopier capacity is being devoted to personal use. If so, he may try to reduce such abuse. Besides guarding and locking the equipment, he may devise procedures for periodically decorating the machine with signs announcing user statistics and unit costs. From time to time he may place an out-of-order sticker on a machine to provide it with respite from its daily disgorgings. He may experiment with various sizes and types of alarms to signal excessive usage, even though this tends to disturb workers in surrounding areas and to trigger footraces to escape detection. If he is admonished for his imaginative but disruptive efforts, he can try to satisfy himself with quieter controls such as rationing the supply of copy paper. But this only encourages the raiding of other agencies' stockrooms, and ultimately a thriving black market in xeropaper.

The supervisor who sets himself up as watchdog of such employee excesses will find that this is not a popular role. Dissident employees will be dedicated to bringing him ridicule. He will find himself caricatured in cartoons on the bulletin boards. Most of the drawings will be distorted and unflattering. A courageous bureaucrat will not be deterred by such critics. After having the xerocopied cartoons removed from display he will reinforce the guard on the copying machines. He will realize that he is dealing with principles bigger than the reproduction equipment itself. To stifle the cartoonists he will remind employees that authorization must be granted for posting anything on the boards, and that any items exhibited must have an official number and be prepared under a valid work authority.

Staff Obstructionists

The staff obstructionists can be useful to an executive who wants to avoid sticking his neck out by making a quick decision. All that he has to do is refer the proposal to them for review and analysis.

Knowing that the best decisions come from the most information, he will wait until all the facts are fully massaged, no matter how long it takes.

A capable bureaucrat will use the administrative employees at all levels to enhance his own position. As long as they are willing to cooperate he will support them and incorporate their monitoring devices into his network of controls. He will alert the file clerks to provide him with copies of useful correspondence and to inform him of any attempts to circumvent the intricately spun webs. The mail sorters will impose control numbers on action documents and make the recipient accountable to the cooperating bureaucrat. His sentries will keep him posted on anything of significance going on anywhere in the agency. When alerted, he will not hesitate to intervene and to impose his authority. In a silent conspiracy the staff will give him service in trade for immunity from his needle.

In addition to such strategically placed collaborators, the supreme bureaucrat may have a dozen agents on his personal staff. They will turn out reams of paper which will make impressive reading for the auditors. They will celebrate a major victory when they find some manager who has overexpended an account by a few dollars, like a disaster supervisor during a flood emergency who spends a little more than his work authorities allow. He will not have time to process the paper during the crisis but nobody will accept that as an excuse. And nobody will add up what it costs for all the sleuths to follow him around while he fights the floodwaters.

The staff functionaries who cluster around a top executive may be handicapped slightly by the fact that the people in the lower echelons do not trust them. There is often good reason for this. The bureau's troops may have taken a close look at the opportunists as they scurried by on their way upward, and therefore may be familiar with their cutthroat tactics.

Correcting Mistakes

Mistakes are sometimes made in the selection of people for government jobs. The supervisor responsible for the correction of such misplacements has a full range of options. At first, until other supervisors raise their guards, he can transfer the misfits to other bureaus. When such opportunities are exhausted he can start shelving them in undemanding positions where they will not be conspicuous. Undoubtedly some of these, because of notorious habits, will be hard to hide.

Dealing with Peers

The government executive must always be sure that others acknowledge his rank. This is not difficult when dealing with outsiders and subordinates. The handling of peers is something else. In calling for a meeting with an equally ranked associate, for example, the bureaucrat should first pit his secretary against the other secretary. If properly trained, the other girl will emphasize that her boss has a very busy schedule and is unable to have a meeting for several days. However, if she can be impressed with the urgency of the call, she may eventually permit a direct telephonic exchange between the two executives. The shrewder man will not pick up the receiver until assured that the other is waiting on the line. When both executives have this same intention, some delay can be

expected before the conversation begins. Once the
connection is made, each man will impress upon
the other the high priority of his current assignments and will emphasize that he is really too busy
to see the other. When these preliminaries are out
of the way, a compromise may be struck by agreeing to meet for lunch on neutral ground. There
should be a mutual commitment to rendezvous at a
precise hour. Upon hanging up, each will likely set
his schedule so that he will be sufficiently late for
the appointment.

The aggressive bureaucrat will intrude into the
territory of others without advance notice, hoping
to catch them off guard. He dare not let secretaries
intercept him. This would cause unnecessary ero-
sion of his status. Once inside the office of a fellow
executive he may show his tendency to take over by
moving chairs, pushing aside objects on the desk
so that he can put his elbows or feet on it, or
dropping whatever he may be carrying on it. Other
gestures which assert superiority within the other's sanctum are the opening and closing of drapes,
sitting on tables, removing one's shoes, or taking
over the telephone for a long call. Any of these
actions may unnerve, disorganize, or even im-
mobilize the competitor in his own territory.

Back in his own office, the aggressor will still
strive to dominate. To impress a visitor with the
importance of his host, incoming telephone calls
can be scheduled so that the visit will be inter-
rupted frequently by callers presumably seeking
counsel. While some visitors may be dismayed by
such intrusion upon their appointed time, most will
be impressed that they are in the presence of a busy
person with considerable influence. It matters not
if the calls come from barber, pawnbroker, or a
prospective handball partner.

In competition among peers, open confrontation should be avoided if possible. Much effective sabotage can be accomplished anonymously. When important meetings are being held, the invitations to rivals can be conveniently misplaced. If they find out about it in time to participate, they may still be inadequately prepared. There may be opportunity also to deprive them of information about deadlines which may be important to the top command.

Caressing the Hierarchy

A conspicuous showing of reverence may be the key to executive favor. Any accomplishment should be shared generously with the bureaucrat overhead. On some occasions, all credit can be relinquished to the superior. Carrying this a step further, the subordinate may quietly offer to assume the least pleasant duties of his boss while still declining any of the credit. Such sacrificial dedication will not go unappreciated. In providing this support, special care must be taken to do everything in the same way the superior would do it if he were energetic. Nothing should be done that would cause any surprises.

The rising subordinate must find out what the top man covets and then give him plenty of it. Once his confidence has been gained, the most threatening competitors should be discussed privately with him, pointing out their weaknesses but assuring the boss that his honorable informant would be big enough to forgive them for their inadequacies. If carefully handled, the chief will see his confidant as the best candidate for advancement. Playing this to the fullest, the aspirant will stage the same performance in several executive-row offices.

The techniques of usurpation are practiced at all levels, and customarily involve ample measures of deception. There are deceivers who take credit for the work of others and thereby cultivate close relationships with people in high places. While they run the most menial errands for the brass, they may brandish viciously any of the authority which rubs off this association. They will chant loudly their support for ideas from on high, making sure that their loyalty and overwhelming esteem for the hierarchy are conspicuous at all times. They will openly condemn those who would challenge the wisdom of the leadership.

To avoid mistakes, the moods of superiors must be sensed carefully. A subordinate who overlooks the behavioral signs can get into trouble fast, as demonstrated in the following example drawn from real experience:

The assistant administrator was feeling low. Nobody had been showing him respect lately. He had to make an example of somebody. He summoned the closest bureau chief.

"You're breaking the rules," he accused.

"What rules?" his victim asked.

"You've set up a security group in direct competition with the Central Service Branch. You should be well aware that you're violating regulations."

"I don't remember a regulation about that."

"Too many people are pleading ignorance of the rules."

"Do you have a copy of that rule?"

"Yes, I do. Right here on my desk. It's clear enough. I don't see how anybody could mistake its intent." The assistant administrator handed over a dog-eared xerocopy of a memorandum.

The bureau chief read it carefully and shook his

head. "This is five years old, addressed from you to the Chief of the Central Service Branch. And I don't see that it applies to security. You just instructed the CSB to coordinate fire drills in the agency."

"Don't tell me what it says . . . You know the CSB is short of work."

"This is out of their line. They're not experts on security."

"That's not the point! The CSB men are here and we have to use them. That's the policy and I expect you to follow it."

"I budgeted my group a long time ago. It went through all the channels."

"I told you I don't want any excuses. You've violated the rule, and I'm not going to drop this without a full investigation."

The bureau chief went back to his office and thought about it. The whole encounter seemed to lack logic. Then he realized what was really bothering the assistant administrator. Nobody had saluted him lately. The bureau chief felt guilty for being so insensitive.

While caressing the wants of the overseer, the seeker of his blessing should not overlook his secretary or administrative assistant. The lady who runs the stronghold for him will have many favors to be traded. She can allow or deny access as may suit her fancy. This may make the difference between five minutes and two weeks in waiting for attention. Since messages must filter through her fingers, she has the power also to influence their interpretation. Through this device alone, she can make or break a subordinate.

Any member of the top executive's personal staff may hold such a club. Its size will depend upon the closeness to the leader. Anybody in doubt about the lieutenant's power should play safe and come to the office with hat in hand. A subservient gesture will gain entry. In more difficult cases, this may equate to groveling. But this is all right. Whatever the requirements, they should be accepted gracefully, at least to the extent that this is feasible from a prostrate position.

The offering of oneself in such fashion may appear more like prostitution than backscratching, but for practical purposes the precise location of the caress really does not matter. Nothing is lost by being attentive to those who deal in bureaucratic advantage. Pride may be abraded, but this is a commodity which cannot be traded anyway.

Acquaintanceship with one or more dignitaries is insurance against disciplinary action by a supervisor placed in between. Each bureaucrat should have at least one protector in a high station to whom he can refer when he wants to straighten out his superior. This instrument, if finely adjusted, can be used either as a weapon or a lure. It does not have to be brandished often. Once the boss gets the message, he will not need reminding, unless the subordinate's purpose is to terrify him.

Even though their powerful stations may be precarious and their stardom fleeting, some politicians are sought after as guests at cocktail parties and as companions in saloons. They are less elusive than some actors and may be more willing to perform for nothing. Lowly bureaucrats who rub their elbows gain instantly in status. Back at the office they can ride high by periodic releases of confidences shared at the bar.

Getting the Money

A large part of governmental endeavor is

devoted to the budget, which gets massaged very thoroughly as it passes through the hands of a multitude of reviewers. Along the way, looking over shoulders, are droves of advocates and auditors representing many interests.

The wizards of bureauland know how to protect themselves at budget time. The budgeter's unwritten set of tactics is voluminous. Primary objectives of the adventurous are to expand in territory and to increase the funding for pet programs. Just to hold ground, some proposed expansion is necessary. Any threat of real budget reduction will generate quick defensive moves by well-trained bureaucrats. Few governmental stimuli will trigger speedier action.

A budget must be prepared for adversary scrutiny. A normal reviewer will total its columns and be stimulated if he finds anything amiss. He will not be satisfied until he does something to justify his role as a critic. To get such role-playing out of the way early in the process, the shrewd budgeter may even plant a slight arithmetic error or two. Some reviewers like to find misspellings. Here again the budgeter may strive to accommodate. Once the obvious flaws are located and removed, the examiner who found them may feel charitable. This will yield benefits when the time for consideration of dollar augmentations arrives.

Proposals for future expenditures usually must be presented at a conference attended by the bureau's top executives. On these occasions, everybody is expected to talk a lot. Custom dictates that budget statements be comprehensive. The more difficult the programs are to understand, the more oratory will be needed for explanation. Unavoidably there will be some attendant risk of confusing the reviewers and of discouraging them from asking questions that might be embarrassing.

In making conference presentations, the psychological effects of bar charting should be fully explored. A high thin bar conveys an impression of everything that is good and moral. A lower and thicker bar has ugly connotations. The color of the budget's cover also may be meaningful to reviewers. Some analysts regard green as indicative of financial integrity. Blue is soothing. Black is disquieting. And red may be outright disturbing. Some American budgeters have experimented with red-white-and-blue covers, but with only mixed results.

Admittedly, the cost of meticulous budget preparation is high, but it yields important benefits. For one thing, it challenges the budget staff to an elevated level of performance. It also confines agency efficiency to more predictable bounds. Without faithfully enforced budgetary criteria, the inevitable changes in trends during the fiscal year would tempt managers to alter their courses to be more responsive to demands. Obviously this could lead to chaos. Some degree of efficiency must be sacrificed to keep the ship of state on a steady bearing. As long as a manager stays within the narrow corridor of budget restraints, he does not have to worry about accountability. Any auditor can measure his performance easily and determine that the dynamics of the changing world have not distorted his program.

The staff officers charged with program analysis will also give some attention to the overhead, focusing especially on the number of supervisors responsible for production. Ratios can be improved by having either fewer supervisors or more employees. The latter is more popular. Some managers who spend the most money have very good overhead percentages. This is another way to please the auditors.

Protecting Territory

If money is budgeted, it must be spent. Prevalence of job vacancies is one of the least desirable conditions in government. It gives the impression that work could be done with fewer people. Every effort should be made to keep positions filled. When an opening occurs, vigorous recruitment should be conducted to close the hole immediately. Critical staffing deficiencies must be eliminated no matter how many recruiters have to be diverted from other work. To make full use of funds, there have to be enough people in the bureau. When in doubt, doubling up on staffing should assure that all work is covered at least once. Occasionally such generous attention to manpower may result in conspicuous overlap, but a little of this will not hurt.

This investment in bureaucratic resources must be defended against infiltration or open invasion. Walls of security have to be built around the bureau. Its secrets must be harbored against rivals. On the other hand, to give the impression of good will and cooperation, cheap information that would be available to anybody with a minimum of investigative effort should be shared generously and conspicuously. In staff meetings, for example, there is profit to be gained by volunteering facts and opinions on any generality that comes to mind—as long as the really valuable data are kept in an inside pocket.

Security and status often go hand in hand.
Neither welcomes change, whether it be new faces,
new rules, or a new set of forms. Being left undis-
turbed is a measure of privileged station. Other
yardsticks, including the job classifications and
the closely related salary levels, can be mislead-
ing. Cosmetics such as office size, reserved parking, and coffee service are indicative, but the grand
prize is insulation from interference. Only a privileged few can have it.

Expanding Territory

The builder of bureaucratic empire must get his
hands on the mechanisms which control money
and information. He must manipulate communication upward to inflate good news and to filter out
the bad. Downward censorship is needed to keep
subordinates in line. With a firm throttle on the
flow of funds and paper, the emperor does not have
to seek much else. Everything will come to him.
The one guideline that he must not forget is that his
own entrenchment has to contribute to the preservation of the bureau. All that he is or will become
must rest on that foundation.

Anybody preparing for a takeover should send
his feelers into the channels to find material helpful to his interests. This requires thorough grinding of the grist that enters the mill. Each minus-
cule detail must be winnowed and sliced and turned
exhaustively. By siphoning off the flowing ideas,
the aggressor can slow up or divert anything that
might benefit the opposition. Also he can document for high-level examination any deficiencies
he finds in his adversary's work.

A more open technique is the use of the

coordinator role for usurpation. In pulling the fragments of an effort together, there are easy opportunities to place a personal stamp on anything that looks good. The judges in executive row will see only the wrappings of the package. They will not know who really deserves the credit. Being the packager also facilitates camouflage of inferior input by the coordinator himself.

An avid bureaucrat will subordinate everybody whom he can reach. His style in usurping the rights and the territory of his brethren may be varied. The tools used to bring underlings into the fold will run the whole gamut from backscratching to coercion. To climb in the hierarchy, the aggressor must probe for points of weakness in the provinces of others. If he finds a weak competitor he must move in on the man's subordinates and demand little things like their weekly schedules and their vacation plans. He should shoot out memoranda of inquiry and offer free advice. He may invite the lieutenants of his rivals to his own staff meetings to establish his control over them. And he may arrange to have the mail of other offices routed to him so that he can reply over his own signature, thereby filing claim to new beachheads. The tactics should be flexible. The whole idea is to get the attention of the troops and make them respond to him. Soon the opposition will be shoved aside and the aggressor can take over.

To gain influence over peers and subordinates of peers, the bureaucrat interested in territorial expansion may do them the courtesy of asking them for complimentary copies of their progress reports and other paper output. Flattered by his interest they may be more than generous in their response. Gradually he can establish his permanent place on

their mailing lists. As time goes on, they may
forget how or why they started reporting to him. In
the beginning, when he offers helpful advice on
their products, they may be appreciative. As the
months go by and they find themselves explaining
their actions to him in response to his frequent
notes and telephone calls, they may wonder what
has happened to them. The fact that he is getting
their attention at all is evidence of the extent of his
growing encroachment.

A bureaucrat who surrounds himself with adequate staff can multiply these intrusions almost
endlessly. The information extracted from many
quarters can be compiled so that the office of the
encroacher becomes the nerve center for information flow in the agency. Anybody who wants to
know anything about happenings in the maze
knows where to turn. The information may come at
a price but it will always be readily available. Even
the original contributors of information may benefit indirectly by having their material returned to
them along with the encroacher's appraisal of their
work. These notes might have been easy to ignore
at the beginning of the encroachment but as time
goes by and the role of the intruder is more widely
accepted, ignoring him will not be so easy. That he
continues to function in his expanding role may be
accepted as evidence that somebody in the hierarchy has given him sanction. Rather than ask
questions, it may seem safer to give him the attention that he demands.

The usurper must call upon all the allies that
he can find. Often these will be fellow usurpers who
are more than willing to trade favors in areas
where they are not in competition. On other occasions, an unwitting accomplice may be used. Some-

times an advisory group will serve this purpose. Consulting boards and commissions may be called upon to give such support. A bureaucentric can dig just about any foothold he wants, and enlarge and reinforce it, by getting his own consultants. He has to make sure that his proprietorship is exclusive. This usually presents no great difficulty. Once his domination is secure he should maximize his advantage by feeding the board a diet of agenda items that orient them properly. If he desires to encroach upon somebody else's area of responsibility, he should ask his board for advice about the work in that sector. Being experts on the technical aspects of the work but perhaps unaware of the subtleties of bureaucratic rivalry, the consultants will not be bound by administrative fences. They will be glad to counsel him on how to run his competitor's territory. He can then distribute their report to his superiors as evidence that his aggressions are justified.

In a real case, the following memorandum was sent by one bureau chief to another:

> At its meeting on January 17, the Consulting Board on Control Systems reported that it was concerned about the practice of your technicians in handling graphic records. It is the Board's understanding that your personnel are permitting the interruption of chart flow. This is regarded by the Board to be a completely unacceptable procedure. Before responding to the Board, I must have your assurance as to the actions which you plan to take to correct this situation. Give me your report no later than January 22.

The receiver of the memo called in an aide. "Look what he's doing to us now," he said. "He owns the Control Systems consultants and he passes them off as an Agency-wide board. Here he is using them to invade our territory."

The aide examined the memo. "The Board is completely wrong about the way we handle the records, but if you respond with the correct information you'll be playing into his hands by subordinating to him. Still, he has the ear of the Administrator. You notice that he sent a carbon copy to him."

The bureau chief called in his secretary and dictated his reply:

> Thank you for your suggestions. Of course, the records to which you refer have had my personal attention since the program was activated. In the opinion of the Administrator and other thoughtful observers who have examined the results, the charting effort has yielded satisfactory data. Since the subject matter is unrelated to your Board's assignment, they can certainly be excused for their mistaken conclusion. To be helpful, I am asking my staff to talk with your consultants to clarify their misconceptions.

He sent a carbon copy to the Administrator.

A government unit may slide from prosperity to depression as the need for its services declines. This is when the bureaucrat in charge may meet his greatest challenge. A sick agency must not be allowed to die. Various kinds of bureaucratic medicine may be prescribed. Obviously, the leader must search for new responsibilities for his group. If access can be gained, one place to look is in the office of the chief executive himself. An endless stream of citizens' advice flows through the headquarters. A beleaguered bureaucrat can offer his talent to resolve the people's concerns. Although work can sometimes be obtained in this way, the problem may be in finding adequate funding. This may call for a bold raid on the moneys assigned to other units.

Financed by these filched funds, the bureaucrat

can take each issue raised by the citizens and develop it into a major problem requiring large-scale investigation by his staff. A single postcard from a lonely voter can trigger a massive effort. Necessarily this may lead deeply into the territory of other bureaucrats, where some usurpation will be imperative. Therefore, the scouting parties should be large and their lengthy reports should avoid giving credit to the jurisdiction of their comrades across the boundary. This is an understandable oversight drawn from a long tradition which pardons theft in the name of survival.

Survival

The bureaucrat who wants to rise to the top and stay there must keep himself unassailable. He should never share his doubts about his own capacity. Any sign of weakness could invite attack. If doubts have to be cast, they should be thrown at others. A bureaucrat who is aggressively wrong can often prevail over one who is timidly right.

Usually, however, the executive will let a trial balloon drift across the horizon before taking himself into a target area. He may even paint somebody else's name on the balloon. If it is shot down he has lost nothing. He may try out his proposals on friendly listeners, rehearsing his arguments until he knows that he can make a sale. In approaching an area where policy is uncertain, a gentle probing of the perimeter is prudent. The password must be carefully selected to convey a bright commitment to whatever the policy may become. In an arena where competitors are wont to jostle for attention of the hierarchical elite, the wise participant will volunteer his views only when he is certain of the

positions of his superiors. He will dodge antag-
onistic challenges rather than be shot down by a
questioner vying for recognition. He may give his
wholehearted support to a proposal in which he has
no vested interest, and at the same time he may
work secretly for its defeat. In this way he can be a
good guy while he's killing off the competition.
Avoidance of open opposition will assist in paint-
ing a positive image.

To protect his flanks, the careful executive will
try to get others to document their commitments
while he only whispers his own promises. However, the written word can sometimes be worked to
advantage, especially when one's own praises
must be sung. Memoranda which do this should be
distributed widely, whether others are interested in
reading them or not. On the other hand, a letter or
memorandum which might be useful to a competitor should be withheld from him if possible. His
name can be left off the routing slip or it can be
placed out of order at the bottom of the list, almost
as an afterthought. Arrangements can be made to
delay it further at the next-to-last desk.

Although he lives in a world flooded with
paper, the bureaucrat must still be extremely careful when he is obligated to put anything into writing. Unless recording devices are operating in the
immediate vicinity, he need not have the same in-
hibition about oral deliveries. Vocalized communication tends to dissolve quickly and lend
itself to retrospective correction. A message
entered on paper, however, may be practically
indestructible, given the government's proclivity
for documentary preservation. Thus, a wary bureaucrat may be generous with the mouth but
stingy with the pen.

The bureaucrat is usually taken seriously by the citizenry and therefore has to work hard to cover his tracks. He will make his share of mistakes but he must not admit them. Others may have to be sacrificed to keep his record clean. Pinning the blame on the administrative staff is an easy way.

Perhaps the most dangerous act that a bureaucrat can commit, aside from kicking the chief executive himself, is to step on the tentacles of the control agencies. Their supremacy is not to be challenged. Anybody who attracts their scrutiny is to be pitied. All the dodging from one side to the other, which may work well with lesser antagonists, will not throw the control agents off the track. Failing in his escape, their quarry can still find consolation in the compassionate treatment granted him in the separation process. He can expect to be given the privilege of resigning and may even receive a distinguished service award upon his departure.

Chapter 5

the
Upper Echelons

Officials at the top levels of the governmental pyramid may view the bureaucracy quite differently from those who reside in the labyrinth. Chief executives and legislative politicians naturally want to use it to further their causes, but somehow few of them have been able to get a handle on it.

The Chief Executive

The survival of the chief executive may be highly dependent upon his relationship with the bureaucracy. If Richard Nixon had been able to keep control of all his subordinates and their subordinates in turn, his place in history might have been quite different. He still would have been at the mercy of the media, but newspaper reporters and television commentators alone could not have brought him down.

Those who hold elective office must learn that their ambitions can be dashed by bureaucrats who prefer cautious analysis to innovative ideas that may threaten the integrity of the system. A wise chief executive must recognize the large investment that the bureaucracy has in the continuation of constancy. It will oppose anything that appears to interfere with this. The flow of money that has been actuated by politics is used by the bureaucracy to sustain itself. Any attempt to turn down the spigot will be met by militant supporters of the endangered agency, including constituencies who have access to the media. An imaginative reporter can quickly turn an economy move into a horrible attack upon the downtrodden of society.

With this kind of support, the bureaucratic machine has been practically unstoppable. Various political leaders have taken it on and have come off second best in the confrontation. Richard Nixon, despite his other troubles, was willing to challenge the entrenched agencies which were supposedly under his command. He saw burgeoning government as a threat to free enterprise and to the economic well-being of citizens in general. Taxes were going up and there appeared to be no way to stop them without trimming the bureaucracy. Nixon soon found that curbing governmental spending habits and draining power away from the bureaus were bigger jobs than he had expected. He came to realize that the bureaucratic monster had not grown by accident, but had been nurtured solicitously by a multitude of constituencies which were not to be denied. For a President who tended to project as a villain even when he had good intentions, the opposition was just too much. Practically every effort to reduce expenditures brought him condemnation as a tyrant who delighted in starving the helpless.

Nixon's proposed solution to the bureaucratic dilemma was to pull in the reins of authority and to run things from the White House. This weakened the status of his cabinet secretaries. It also gave him a problem that he did not expect, that of locating where the power really was, so that he could pull it in. To cope with this he laid plans for planting his loyalists within the bureaucracy. These met with only spotty success, since they were easily recognizable. The bureaucratic arm of government quickly turned its constituencies and the press against them. If Nixon had left well enough alone, the balance of power in Washington might have sustained him. By attempting to unbolt the bureaucratic machine, he got caught up in the gears and was ground up brutally. In reaching for power, at least he found out where it really was.

Ascent into the hierarchy lengthens the tubes through which information flows. Those at the lower end may know what is wrong but their ideas, which tend to rise by osmosis, may never reach the top in understandable form. The chief executive is highly dependent on others to show him the way. The information that he receives is screened and rationed. If he were to strive to learn by probing on his own, he would soon find that his access to the facts was quite limited. He will usually be told only what others want him to hear.

Concentric circles of power are drawn around the chief executive. A small ring at the center insulates the exalted from the multitude and may shape policy even when the leader would just as soon do it himself. The man or woman who occupies a key post at the hub will naturally accumulate enough authority to do the job well. A kindly chief executive will allow such freedom of action in the inner circle. The aides who protect him from intrusions must have power. They have to brandish his name fearlessly when other weapons fail. While the chief may sanction this assumption of power by his immediate staff, he cannot be sure when it may be used to excess. Anybody trying to get through to him from outside must accept the filtration of inbound and outbound messages. The outsider may never know whether, or in what form, the word got through to the center. And the chief, perhaps unaware of the presence or the problem of the caller, is left to weigh policy on the basis of the information delivered to him by the gatekeepers.

Richard Nixon used Bob Haldeman as his guard at the door, insulating himself from those who would press him to make decisions or to grant favors. He could relay his ideas through this sentinel without worrying that they would represent commitments. The fence that Nixon built around himself with Haldeman as the gatekeeper was nearly impenetrable and this was the way the President wanted it. Even his personal secretary was kept at arm's length. While this rubbed Rose Mary Woods painfully, Haldeman did not mind being the villain with her or anybody else. He appreciated the importance of defending the President from intrusion and he guarded the gate zealously.

Haldeman was motivated by more than his fierce loyalty to the President. His style of operation demanded that he prevent end runs by those who wanted access to the oval office of the White House. He coached the presidential staff that bypassing of channels was a cardinal sin. Those who surrounded him at the White House were promised that he would permit them to see the President when it was absolutely necessary, in his judgment. He justified his rigorous gatekeeping on the basis that the President's time had to be saved for the highest priorities. To make this system effective, all written communications had to flow through Haldeman's office and be examined there to see if they were worth moving forward.

Even when access was gained into the inner chamber, the rules required that somebody be present to take notes on what was said. While Haldeman was seen as the policeman who insisted upon such measures, he was only doing what Nixon wanted. With this kind of policing, nobody had a chance of catching the President at a weak moment and getting him committed to something that he would regret later. Haldeman reportedly also kept an eagle eye on him through various devices, such as watching the telephone console to see whose light was on when the President was speaking. He also used spies to alert him when end runs were made despite the barricades that he had set up. He did not hesitate to hasten to the President's office if he discovered that some intruder had gained entry. Haldeman's power at the White House was applied both to incoming and outgoing communication. With the President's blessing, he served as interpreter and conveyor of the President's thinking. He studied Nixon's viewpoints carefully and parceled out his knowledge to the staff as he saw appropriate.

Needless to say, a position in the inner circle carries with it splendid opportunities for helping or hindering the objectives of those who come to

the gates. Denial of access, or communicative dis-
tortion, can destroy missions and reputations. Just
as easily, hopes can be realized and images
enhanced—if the staff chooses to give its blessing.

Communication between the chief executive
and the lower echelons can always stand improvement. The simplest message can lose its meaning
as it wends its way through the channels. A casual
inquiry by the chief about the fishing conditions at
a favorite resort may activate comprehensive
investigations and statistical analyses by the agencies involved in fish and wildlife programs. The
underling who inherits the job of drafting the final
report may wonder exactly what he is expected to
do, but it would be too long a route back up through
the channels to ask the chief if he just wanted to go
fishing.

Sometimes the viscosity in communications
may be attributed simply to bad morale. Where this
is suspected some effort should be made to cheer
people up. The chief can delegate this task to one of
his subordinates, giving him full purview over
agency morale and demanding to see some quick
results. Most conscientious lieutenants will
respond to this challenge and may ponder the problem for days on end. Often as not, however, the
issue of morale will eventually be returned to the
head man. In the solitude of his spacious office with
the door closed, he may do some pondering himself, trying to find a way to reach his people. Those
who would venture into the employee workrooms
may find an answer. After all, the leaders still have
to talk to the masses.

Despite his insulation, the man on top can
make his will felt among the people in the ranks. If
he is interested in discipline he can turn to the

Basic Services Agency to whip the troops into line. With its special talents in regimentation of the masses, the BSA can transmit the command without emotional distortions. Using the impassive control agency as intermediary has the advantage of stratifying discontent. The chorus of tiny complaints from the workrooms will be filtered out in the long channel via the BSA to the chief executive, who might sympathize if given full exposure.

To get the bureaucrats on his side, the chief executive should try to understand what turns them on. For instance, some of the leaders in the maze like publicity, as long as it is flattering. To encourage public respect, there should be ample display of bureaucratic accomplishments at all government facilities. In addition to monuments and billboards and plaques, exhibits should be offered to tell something about the government's officials as individuals. The people have a right to know who the men are who administer vital projects. There should be liberal use of photographs. The exhibit of portraits of leaders is a universally accepted practice. Each picture should have an appropriate caption and a biographical sketch. The whole gallery should be done in good taste with hardwood display cabinets and plate glass. The public deserves first quality.

Another way to generate respect for the government's doings is to distribute stories to the media. Public relations specialists are numerous in government. There are reported to be more than fifteen hundred people handling the news in the Department of Defense. Runner-up position is occupied by the Department of Health, Education and Welfare, which is said to have more than one thousand. The Department of Agriculture has only about six hundred, according to an unofficial count.

With these helpers, a bureaucrat can stage an event that attracts newsmen, such as a conference on recreation, held at a mountain resort or at the seashore. He can invite a few hundred guests, including a few politicians and other celebrities. A caravan of photographers can be assigned to travel with the party, shooting scenes each step of the way. As a useful by-product, the bureaucrat can have a film featurette made dealing with some of his personal efforts. This can include chatty interviews with some of his friends and associates, spliced in with some of the outdoor footage. Special attention should be given to the musical background of the film.

A bureaucrat will place high value on his public information officer, who is paid to tell the citizens what they are entitled to know about the official's successes. To accomplish this, the press relations specialist will try to (1) mention his superior in every seventh sentence of each news release; (2) build up suspense by announcements that his man will make an important revelation on a given date; (3) encourage encounters between public officials and have the participants plan this together, since the news benefits may accrue to both; (4) create interest if possible by inviting dissidents to public meetings, and by cooperating with reporters to intensify excitement; (5) maximize all numbers by using factors, converting tons and miles to ounces and inches; and (6) preserve credibility by being honest.

Most agency leaders get concerned from time to time about the condition of their government and want to project a new image. To energize the creative spirit of employees in the bureaucracy a massive rally can be held where the chief can deliver a speech calling for new attitudes. All available speech writers should be put to work on this. The message to the masses should cover every one of the problem areas. Solutions will probably require the formation of numerous task forces. These should be big groups of maybe twenty or thirty people each, to be sure of getting the widest possible participation.

While the task forces are convening, the chief himself can do some reorganizing to strengthen the management. In many cases this may require the appointment of more assistants and deputy assistants for bureau chiefs. In some departments, changing the titles of executives may provide some improvement. After all, they cannot expect their employees to change unless they themselves are willing to change. To get the ranks to take the reform seriously it should be written into the regulations. This will guarantee stability in policy, until the next reorganization.

Following the traditional pattern, an array of advisory bodies will be appointed to study organizational problems in depth. Their numerous and lengthy conferences and trips will be well covered by the media as the many months go by. When the results of their deliberations are finally delivered, the chief will expect his public relations specialists to give them the fullest treatment. He will realize that he must make a decision eventually. Following precedent, such decisions usually raise the center of gravity of the organization.

A threat of major reorganization always stiffens the resistance of the bureaucracy. Battle lines are drawn between the pinnacle of the pyramid and its base. Those at the bottom immediately close ranks to employ their greater experience in governmental processing. Their control of the machinery is tightened. The management may push buttons and pull levers, but the gears may not respond. Everything may slow down as calculated process complication takes hold.

Bureaulings will use their proprietary knowledge of governmental regulations and procedures to accumulate a conspicuous backlog of work as evidence that the system cannot do without them. At the same time they will dodge accountability for malperformance by blaming it on those rules. The political overseers and the public have no easy means of proving otherwise. There is little question, though, that the paper mill would speed up if employees were guaranteed not to lose their jobs as a consequence.

Any agency can stand a good reorganization once in a while. Although this may not have been a panacea in the past, an overhaul each four years may be unavoidable due to the election process. Often, too, there is a need for a shake-up between elections to correct the effects of the four-year restructuring. A lot can go wrong in the interim. When problems do not lend themselves to ready solution, the possibility of their elimination through reorganization should not be overlooked. Some observers would argue that this should be confined to the problem areas, since some bureaus need reshaping more than others. Of course, this would be playing favorites. All parts of the agency should be treated the same. Even though this may seem like inventing problems so that they can be solved, it is the way that it has always been done. Something worth doing is worth doing comprehensively. To be serious about it, though, a realistic observer would have to concede that trying to rejuvenate an aging bureau by changing its name or moving the boxes in the organization chart provides only temporary therapy. Bureaucratic sclerosis is not easily cured by cosmetic surgery.

While a chief executive may find the bureaucracy unresponsive, he can sometimes do better with the lawmakers. A dependable devotee of the game of reciprocity will know how to get the vote of a key legislator to dip his wick into the treasury vaults. A likely way to gain favor is to establish a new regional office in the legislator's district with a substantial payroll of government employees. Commercial interests within his constituency will be delighted when he votes in support of the requested funds. There is nothing wrong with this kind of harmonizing if the office is really needed.

Any bureaucrat with legislative allies is likely to enjoy a long tenure. A friend in the gilded chambers may be worth as much as one in the executive mansion. In fact, chief executives tend to come and go but legislative chieftains and career bureaucrats who give them access to the labyrinth may have few worries about longevity.

Appointed bureaucrats have a special problem of survival. Being the only members of the institution openly vulnerable to dismissal, they must possess refined talents for staying in favor. In devoting their most nervous hours to this endeavor they must manifest a rich blending of genuinely staunch loyalty to the appointing power while avoiding deadly confrontation with warriors with high kill ratios. By using these skills to perfection some political appointees have even survived the departure of their sponsoring hierarchy.

A stellar survivor of this warfare was Secretary of State Henry Kissinger, who is credited with developing the news leak into a fine art. (Whether he deserved this reputation is still debated.) Some observers saw this as one of his most effective weapons in intragovernmental conflict. The pattern of leakage artistry which he allegedly perfected has become standard operating procedure. The first bureaucrat in the game lets loose a small squirt of information which he thinks will help him. His opposition then issues a couple of squirts of balancing leakage. The greatest hazard is that the squirts may become a stream, and muddy at that. When a congressional committee's report on the nation's intelligence system was leaked to the press, Secretary Kissinger attacked Congress's negligence vigorously. At about the same time, fragments of the same information oozed out from the cracks in his own office and he offered indignant defenses. The level of such indignation evidently depends upon who is the leaker and who is the leakee.

The Politicians

While some bureaucrats may not regard politicians as brethren, they have to accept that the money flows through the legislative chambers. To stay in business, the bureau must persuade the lawmakers to keep the faucets running. The politician must be prepared for the bureaucratic money-getters. A newly elected legislator may be inadequately equipped to understand and deal with the bureaucratic baloney that pours into his office. He must delegate the examination of agency propaganda to subordinate analysts who are highly specialized and may not always compare notes.

The new politician may not be able to integrate the data output from these individual staff workers into anything representing an overall analysis. To fulfill his obligations to his fellow legislators and to his constituency, he must concentrate on specialized committee activity where his knowledge can be best applied. When legislative committeemen get together, as they do regularly in the U.S. Congress, they must lean on each other cooperatively to endorse programs which may be quilted together from many separate efforts. This is sometimes advantageous to the bureaucracies, whose sensitive interfaces and intricate programs might be vulnerable to intense scrutiny.

Government workers themselves are a powerful force at the polls. There are nearly three million civilian employees of the federal government alone. Politicians recognize this as an important constituency at election time. The Congress usually does what it reasonably can to be fair to the bureaucracies.

In return for the attention given to it by the Congress, the bureaucracy tries to be fully responsive to the desires of any member of the legislative body. Responding to a questionnaire from one Congressman, for example, the Securities and Exchange Commission produced a two thousand page report plus large stacks of exhibits at a cost of about $100,000. While this was a comparatively modest investment in cooperation, its simple multiplication by the number of such inquiries per year will provide one indicator of harmony's value in government.

Some bureaucrats also work more directly in support of their favorite politicians. Despite the Hatch Act, which was intended to control political activity by civil servants, more than a few natives of the labyrinth do what they can to assure the continuance in power of friendly officeholders. It includes supplying useful information for the campaigns, supportive of the candidate or detrimental to his opponent. This is sometimes risky, particularly if the favorite loses the race.

Power in Washington, D.C., as in most centers of government, is proportioned primarily among the legislative, executive, and bureaucratic arms. However, some historians would say that the Congress in the past has not always had the cohesion to compete effectively for power. Some biased observers even contended that a few legislators were discomforted by authority which obligated them to understand issues, to analyze their long-term effects, and to make correct decisions that might sacrifice votes. Such legislators were accused of preferring to take histrionic approaches to national issues, with a view toward enhancing their press coverage. Their names were placed on the output of their staffs, who were said to be the real authors of the laws that they proposed. This criticism was undoubtedly exaggerated. Certainly the typical Congressman today is a well-informed participant in the process of government. Any bureaucrat who thinks otherwise should take another look.

Under the watchful scrutiny by Congress, the executive and bureaucratic arms have to cope with the people's problems on a daily basis. The roles of the two are well defined. The chief executive is the advocate and the bureaucracy is the one that sets the pace. A President who wants to accomplish must therefore deal with the bureaucratic mechanism while he shares responsibility with the Congress.

In the interest of fairness, even a severe critic must admit that most politicians are good-hearted. The generosity of the Congress has been a bright example to receivers throughout the land. Even though the nation has been so deeply in debt that it can hardly afford to fund the interest thereon, legislators are still willing to dispense tax money to those who appear to be needy. They not only have provided vast sums for disbursement directly to the citizenry but in recent years have hit upon the idea of sharing revenue with the lower levels of government. This courageous plan is being carried out even though the federal treasury may have little to share. The government, however, has been impressively inventive in circumventing this deficiency. All that is required is the printing of more money. Government in the lower echelons from Albany to Honolulu has been an enthusiastic receiver of this beneficence and readily supports the necessary expansion of the federal disbursing agencies.

The legislators in Washington deserve a little sympathy as they contemplate the bureaucracy. For instance, anybody should be able to appreciate the dilemma of the Congress as it tries to cope with the sprawling postal system. Until somebody decides whether it should be run as a business or a public service, it is not likely to function well as either. Critics have suggested that one way to vitalize it would be to give it competition, to take away its exclusive hold on mail delivery. But this certainly would be no way to treat a bureaucracy. The problems of the postal service are well known. Its difficulties are constantly being aired before Congress, which would like to see postal expenses reduced. Evidently this can only be accomplished through curtailment of service or layoffs of workers. The postal unions, however, are ready to remind the Congress that their labor contracts contain provisions against layoffs. They stand ready also to advise on the pitfalls of proposals such as computerizing mail delivery workloads to assure that each letter carrier has no more or less than a full day's work. Again, protection against such idealistic concepts is contained in the union's contract.

Every campaigning official will seek support in the large group of government workers in his constituency. He can be expected to praise the public employees as first-rate in every way and to deplore their treatment as third-class citizens. He will commend the employee unions for their statesmanship, assuring them of his affection. The civil servant masses may shrug this off as quickly as they would any word of good will from his opponent. They have a special resistance which makes them wary of overtures from public officials, regardless of party affiliation.

Political arithmetic is simple. The number of supporters must be maximized while the ranks of the dissenters are reduced to a minimum. This may mean that controversy should be avoided unless sentiment among the constituency bends heavily toward one side of the issue. An elected official who is less than courageous can create the illusion of entering a fight while actually remaining on the fence. For example, he can vote for tighter controls over industrial abuses if he can assure corporation lobbyists that the legislation has no real enforcement teeth. In such cases, he will rely strongly upon bureaucratic viscosity to slow any change to an acceptable rate. If legislation can be passed out without implemental guidelines, the burden of carrying out avowed political intent will rest upon administrative agencies, in whose lower tiers the vote may not matter a lot. When nothing happens, the people will find nobody to blame.

After all is said and done, the bureaucracy is the main force that stands in the way of change. If there were some way that elected representatives could deal with the nation's problems in meditative insulation from everyday anxieties, the burdens of the bureaucracy would be easier to carry. But the system will not allow this. As long as ascent to the peaks of government is dependent on the packaging of popular products, the incumbents on those pinnacles will have difficulty in meeting the real needs of government.

This is where the tenured bureaucrats come in. By contrast, they will not jump nervously each time the electorate raises its voice. They will be calm and unhurried and even indifferent when the occasion demands. The bureaucracy is the essential element which guarantees that there will always be a tomorrow.

Chapter 6

Bureaucracy and the Public

Much has been said about the impact of bureaucracy on civilization. The people have placed their lives in the hands of the regulators and have accepted the discipline to support this trust. The rain of authority falls on every roof.

And the rainfall is heavier than it was in the old days. As result of the Watergate affair, more power has been shifted to the regulatory agencies, which are seen by the people as relatively untainted. The appointees in charge of these bureaucracies are forced to live up to this image unless they want to face attacks from probing reporters or dissident members of their own staffs. Appetites of investigators everywhere have been whetted by the sensational successes of those who exposed the President and his cohorts. Nowadays elected officials and their close followers cannot take chances. If the citizenry wants them to enforce the law, that is the way it will be.

As a matter of fact, though, the intensified activities of the enforcers preceded the troubles of Richard Nixon. The list of major regulatory agencies in the United States increased 100 percent in the ten-year period between 1965 and 1975, and the number of their employees and the costs kept pace. One measure of the rate of expansion is the Code of Federal Regulations, which comprises the basic standing rules enforced by the government. Its finely printed pages number in the many thousands and have been increasing at a rate of 20 percent each year. A study conducted by the Library of Congress disclosed that during 1974 the U.S. Congress enacted 404 laws. At the same time federal agencies issued 7,496 new or amended rules.

The Federal Register has been regarded as one of the government publications most difficult to read. It is the publishing outlet five days a week for official notices, executive orders, and bureaucratic regulations. In 1936 it contained 2,411 pages. Its total number of pages in 1975 was about sixty thousand. Many of these were devoted to publication of the latest rules and rates established during the year. All government agencies have their proposed regulations entered in the Register, so that the people can see what is in the works for them.

Citizens traditionally regard their government as omnipotent. In a sense, it is indeed capable of anything. Considering the great wealth which is continuously poured into its fuel tanks, the high expectations of the people are not unreasonable.

Government bureaucracy has always stood ready to meet the challenge of new crises. However, because of its preoccupation with comprehensive administration of existing laws, the emergence of a new problem must sometimes be called to its attention. Once convinced of the magnitude of the crisis, battalions of bureaucrats will march into action with public hearings and analyses. Numerous agencies will have immediate interest in some fragment of the problem and will start turning out papers dealing with it. Eventually some of these groups will meet on common ground and begin to weigh their interferential responsibilities. Inevitably this will lead to the establishment of committees and the parceling out of assignments. Inherent governmental redundancy will usually offer several layers of agencies to participate, so that unforeseen contingencies will be adequately covered.

Any objective observer would concede that the government is willing to involve itself in any of the affairs of its citizens, from the kinds of insulation and plumbing in homes to the size of exit signs in public facilities. Infestations of mistletoe, for example, could be left to the property owners to combat, but even this parasite is getting governmental attention. In many communities the men of the public agencies patrol neighborhoods searching it out. Control of the blight is seen as a necessary regulatory responsibility. This is only one of thousands of functions that the alert government sentinels have brought into their purview.

Several agencies and levels of government may be involved in a given problem. If the people of a town need help with their garbage, each stratum of government should be given opportunity to participate. The town council and the county board of supervisors and the state legislators from the district will all have legitimate interests. They deserve a part in solving the problem. This takes time. Even though the garbage could be cleaned up in a few days, the governmental process moves at a different rate. Many public hearings and press conferences may be necessary. The testimony of witnesses must be recorded. Reports must be prepared. During such proceedings the comprehensive verbalizing of an implied commitment, if some form of commitment is unavoidable, may be projected with a harmonious blending of wholehearted sincerity and humility. This may take many months. After that the garbage can be cleaned up quickly, including that accumulated in the interim.

Standing outside looking in, some of the bureau's customers may tend to suffer varying degrees of helplessness. They expect to find human interfaces where personal problems can get sensitive treatment. What they do not see is that the system itself is an inhuman apparatus. It meets each demand with impersonal detachment and allows it to trickle through the filters at a prescribed rate.

The people still get what they ask for from government. Bureaucracy is nurtured by the public's apparent desire for massive controls to guarantee that the free enterprise system will not be free. To enforce compliance by the private sector many government agencies have been formed, nearly always with overlapping responsibilities. Frictional interaction among surveillance units stimulates competitive treatment of suspects and a few impediments to coherent policy. Inevitable disorder in the ranks of the investigators tends to confuse those being watched. The diverse demands of the many surveillants assure that each quarry will be adequately disquieted so that he will measure painstakingly his future contributions to the nation's economy. There will be plenty of time for this while last year's problems are filtered through the bureaucratic screen. The dedicated governmental ruminators may move slowly so that all the critics will come forward to join the attack. People of commerce who wade through the successive firing lines of a multitude of investigating agencies find themselves supremely challenged and therefore may come out the better for it. Granted, some lesser applicants for officialdom's blessing may fall by the wayside, discouraged and even defeated by preachment, paperwork, and postponement. But those who weather the jungle's trials are worthy survivors who can build a stronger society. The same defenders who called for inquisition will decry the demise of the weaklings and the consequent undermining of competition in the market place. They would eat their cake and save it too. There is no way for the bureaucracy to please them entirely. The amorphous retarder is never popular.

As government participates ever more widely in the enterprises of its citizens, inevitably compliance with official orders will be slow. Those scrutinized and controlled will have difficulty in understanding the new edicts. Many companies are now establishing full-scale divisions of people of high rank to assure proper response to government programs. Specialists have to be hired to interpret the regulations. Lawyers particularly are in increasing demand to translate the government's wishes. These translations are often helpful to the regulators themselves. Other kinds of specialists must be recruited and assigned to conversion of the governmental word into revised procedures in the shops. The scramble to develop and disseminate analyses of the multitudinous new laws has fostered the rise of whole new groups of disciplines in government and in other sectors. The older regulatory institutions have found new breath of life in the trends set by the creation of new competitive bureaucracies. They are moving ahead vigorously, unwilling to be outdone in the race to satisfy the people's desire to be more strongly controlled.

Criticism

Regulatory agencies are accused often of usurping authority to satisfy the wants of the residents of the government chambers. This is an affront to dedicated civil servants, who are just trying to serve the needs of the people as seen from the bureau's elevated vantage point. Regulators who impose severe demands on the applicants who come before them are only setting high standards, which are not always as arbitrary and superfluous as some malcontents have charged. Those who would criticize must understand that any function of government has to protect its public image. Everything must be done cautiously to ensure pleasant circumstances in the bureau. Those who administer the laws must be wary of experimentation with new ideas. Innovation has to be based upon unquestioned need. In most cases, old and established methods will yield at least approximate solutions to new problems.

From time to time, Congress does cast a look at the regulatory bureaucracies and makes gentle gestures toward reform. Such attention will usually stir the scrutinized agency into agitated righteousness. This is when the heaviest rocks are thrown at the companies under purview. Much commotion may be generated before Congress's fist is lowered, and the traditional regulators settle back into their well-worn chairs.

That the government can be responsive to the needs of the citizenry was well demonstrated in 1976 when President Ford issued his plea for elimination of unnecessary regulations and paperwork. His chief lieutenants traveled to every corner of the country to bring firsthand word of the government's responsiveness. Regional conferences were held to improve communication and to lay the groundwork for the elimination of confusion. Agencies spent many months drafting plans to explain themselves. Some agencies even reorganized to a limited extent and established new high-level executive positions to take charge of improving communication channels with the public.

While such stirrings demonstrate that government leaders are concerned, some citizens want more than that. Those who see bureaucracy as bad will point to the geometric multiplication of unproductive rules and regulations in America. They point to the impact of minimum-wage laws on teenagers and minorities. They say that through federal aid to dependent children the government has financed illegitimacy. They direct attention to the number of people employed by regulatory agencies and to the rapidly expanding expenditure of money for such purpose. They charge that the regulatory bureaucracy is expanding faster than the industries under its purview. Examples that are cited are the Federal Communications Commission, which allegedly impedes technological advancements, and the Federal Power Commission, (superseded recently by the Federal Energy Regulatory Commission) which, among its other achievements, is believed by some critics to have fostered a national shortage of natural gas through its pricing policies. Some citizens unwilling to acknowledge the benefits of big government argue that such agencies are depriving the American consumer of the right to make his own decisions.

Constituencies

Faced with such criticism, a bureau must cultivate ever-expanding constituencies who will rise readily to its support at a given signal. The supporters of the agency must be showered with free and ample services, and must be informed fully of the agency's benevolent role in the supply of favors. In spreading the word about itself the agency cannot afford to be modest. No real harm will be done, in fact, if its public relations specialists manage to put its label on somebody else's work. They will emphasize the magnificence of the bureau's achievements. This alone will tax their imaginations, since the bureau's attainments in any given year may consist entirely of spending its full budget. In fact, most government agencies measure their accomplishments by comparing planned expenditures versus actual outlay. By some standards, underexpenditure is synonymous with failure. An agency which reverts funds at the end of the fiscal year must be regarded as a failure, while the bureau which begs for more money must be seen as energetic and worthy of attention. In asking for a larger helping of the pie, a bureau must call attention to the expanding services that it renders to society, even though its real area of service may be limited. It can depend on the continuing support of the beneficiaries of its services in those areas. Its public relations efforts, therefore, must be bent toward persuasion of taxpayers and politicians beyond the reach of its generous sprinklings. They must be convinced somehow that the bureau is doing them some good, even if it is not. If its goodness is not apparent, its badness must certainly be obscured. This communicative exercise is the stock in trade of the public relations staff. These are people of immense talent who are worth their weight in disappearing dollars.

Yardsticks for measuring the benefit-cost ratios of agencies involved in social therapy cannot be precise. Only a very presumptuous auditor would suggest that such agencies pay their own way. The justification for their existence would dissolve. Practically nobody seeks to buy bureaucratic services. There are only distributors and receivers. Those who pay are on the outside, sometimes sadly bewildered. They are the givers, and they may have little hope of changing the system by which government perpetuates itself through redistribution of the wealth. This will change only when there are not enough givers to go around.

A noteworthy aspect of the relationship between a bureaucrat and his clients is that they are both receivers. Yet they are not competitive. In fact they are interdependent. The client can't get his unless the bureaucrat gets his at the same time. The people who gain from the bureau's existence must be served continuously even while the bureau adjusts its functions to assure its survival. If properly nurtured, these constituencies will offer unsagging support even after the agency has completed its original mission and could pack its bags and fade away. Of course, whatever the bureau dispenses to its constituencies must be given at a discount, if it isn't entirely free. Nobody will turn away from a benefactor who remembers this.

The bureaucracy serves multitudes of narrow interests which in sum total may not represent the majority of the people. This may not be of paramount concern to some bureaucrats if the most vocal and influential constituencies are satisfied and the positions of those in government are strengthened. Those who would decry a disproportionate allocation of governmental favor may be reminded that the real need is to serve those who ask to be served.

Attorneys at law are essential cogs in government everywhere. Each new law that flows from the legislative mill makes more work for lawyers. The multitudinous ranks of the legal profession in the government echelons are not only necessary but must be continuously replenished. To assist in this, there is a Federal Council on Legal Educational Opportunity charged with the funding of federal scholarships for those who aspire to become members of the bar. Nit-picking critics have suggested that the market is already saturated with attorneys. This, of course, ignores the need for legal interpreters to serve the common man as legislative disgorgings become increasingly complex.

Public Exposure

While lawyers may tie their knots in quiet corners, other civil servants prefer the excitement of public exposure. To assure that bureaucratic accomplishments get proper notice and evaluation, each government body will issue reports periodically. Traditionally these are greeted with enthusiasm and ceremony. The officials will hold news conferences and have their photographs taken. Key figures may appear on television and allow themselves to be interviewed in an entertaining fashion. Even if a report suggests some overhauling of government policy, nobody will be very disturbed. The publication of the findings will demonstrate to the populace that its government is alert and willing to examine the possibilities of change. A basic obligation is therefore fulfilled by issuance of the report. There is not much more that the responsible body can do. Most of its ideas may require legislative processing, the outcome of which is unpredictable. If there is general consent to air the findings in public hearings, a long period of deliberation will follow, during which many voices will be heard and reams of records will be printed for the archives. The regulators and the regulated will grapple for position while the electorate can rest assured that nothing will happen fast.

Statistics

In a democracy the citizens have a right to be informed. This calls for statistics. Stacks and stacks of data are compiled so that trends can be measured. Without statistics the people could see that prices, taxes, crime, and government cost were going up, but they would not know precisely how much. To boil the great volumes of figures down into something useful, various agencies have attempted to calculate statistical indices. In case a citizen cannot sense what is going on in his own neighborhood, he can at least take comfort in reading the state and national yardsticks.

Statistics are vital in the administration of government programs. For example, they may determine whether or not federal funds are disbursed for a given purpose. The rate of unemployment calculated by the government is used as a gauge to measure the amount of subsidy flowing to the jobless in a given vicinity. The consumer price index variations trigger increases in the money flow to not only the recipients of federal benefits but also to those whose income is indexed to the government's statistics. Official indices can be interpreted in so many ways that those forecasters who use them are left with plenty of options. The hedging of economic forecasts, for example, enables readers to make their own choices.

Bureaucrats keep a close watch on the economic indices, claiming what credit they can for uptrends and ducking the blame for declines. They may even influence them if given an opportunity. Knowing that statistics on housing starts would be released just two weeks before the presidential election of November 1976, the Secretary of Housing and Urban Development reportedly urged lieutenants to accelerate federally insured and subsidized apartment projects in September, thus enhancing statistical protection of the incumbency.

Of course, measuring the true output of public programs is most difficult. The desire to provide such measurement has resulted in a proliferation of indices for every kind of government activity. Most administrators see the need for interpretation of the paper being vomited from their machines, and they have done their best to be responsive. In the government warehouses there are rooms full of interpretive publications, stored next to the supporting data volumes. All of these in turn are indexed for reference.

The federal government has served as a model for most other compilers of statistics. Funded by an apparently unlimited taxing capacity it has pio-

neered in the most complex systems and has therefore developed an expertise which it shares generously with local aspirants. The government
distributes from its vast warehouses multitudinous bundles of printed wisdom. But to learn the
ropes and how they are braided requires a firsthand examination of agency activities in the
nation's capital. To follow the federal example, several commissions and councils should be set up to
examine the indicators and to issue evaluative reports. A commission on statistical studies should
be established to report on which further government reports are needed. In general, data on government output do need improvement. If the available results were taken at face value the average
man in the street could only conclude that production by government agencies is lagging. Obviously the analytical techniques need refinement.

The manipulative potential in common statistical analysis provides flexibility in arriving at
conclusions. Data sometimes can be adjusted
through application of variable coefficients. Some
analysts would say that there is no sense in using
statistics unless they can serve a useful purpose.
Nobody wants to be bored by monotonous disgorgings of uncorrelated data. The conforming of
statistics to governmental objectives requires
specialists who have a full depth of understanding
of the interdependence of numerical and human
factors. These experts are so valuable that they
may be isolated from everyday activities and allowed to meditate without interference, except by
those to whom they must be responsive.

The National Commission on Supplies and
Shortages spent a year or more in analysis of what
causes material shortages. It found that govern-

ment itself was one of the prime culprits. During the period 1972-74 the federal government had tried its hand at controlling prices and exports. At the same time it was venturing ever more deeply into social reform such as consumer and environmental protection and worker safety. While the bureaucracy knew little about any of these, it knew least about manipulating the economy. The commission found that certain government actions had stimulated consumer demand while at the same time discouraging investment in production facilities. Perhaps unnerved by its discovery, the commission followed the safe tradition of scheduling public hearings. Having thus assured a long-term program of discussion and analysis, the commission did not recommend specific changes in the role of government related to material shortages. It did realize that the government needs to be better educated on the functioning of the economy. It suggested therefore that the makers of decisions somehow be made better informed. The tentative findings of the commission did not cause much of a stir since American business had been accommodating uninformed bureaucratic actions for a long time. There was no reason to think that it couldn't adjust to a few additional interferences.

Reporting

The federal government also has a Paperwork Management Office (PMO) which is intended to encourage reduction in paperwork. One of the devices used by the PMO is an annual contest among cutters of red tape. Contest instructions are reportedly lengthy. Each nomination form must be filed in sextuplicate. This consumes a lot of paper. The PMO necessarily has impressive files to document who saves the most. It has set an example that has drawn attention not only in the labyrinth but throughout the business world as well. Following this guidance, the American Bankers Association in 1976 confined its testimony to the Commission on Federal Paperwork (CFP) to one solitary page. This proud achievement was made known through a two-page press release.

The CFP was established in 1975 to ease the pain of federal paperwork. Its immediate action was the distribution of a five-page single-spaced request for information on paperwork excesses. The commission wanted businessmen to tell how much government questionnaires were costing them. After many months of analysis, the CFP was only a little closer to the answer. And this should not be surprising, in view of the size of the study area. There are reported to be in excess of eight thousand record systems kept by the federal agencies. These constitute perhaps 100 billion pages. Many thousands of new regulations are added by the federal regulatory agencies each year, and a large number of these involve the filling out of forms.

Regulatory paperwork is said to be stifling and even killing some companies. One big petroleum enterprise submits about one thousand reports each year to thirty-five federal bureaucracies. While this corporation is powerful enough to survive, and gets little sympathy, the costs must be passed on to the customer. Federal regulation alone reportedly cost the consumer about $130 billion in 1976. Eliminating it would put more meat and beans on the average citizen's dinner table, but a lot of bureaucrats would face a lower standard of living.

At one time fifteen different major federal

agencies were circulating 145 questionnaires related to energy. These called for an estimated 11 million responses. Those critics who have argued that such paperwork requirements are just too much have found that the sponsors of questionnaires have a strong constituency, including the makers of printed forms and file cabinets.

The game of filling in the blanks is popular with government agencies at all levels. A typical farmer in California, for instance, must fill out about forty government forms annually. The state requires a large aluminum company to file more than forty different reports each year, involving about a thousand transmittals and the full-time services of a paperwork specialist.

The California Health and Welfare Agency has been rated as the champion bureaucracy in that state. This distinction has been earned through diligent use of the questionnaire by nineteen separate units in the Department of Health. A 263-question form must be filed with the Department each year by more than one hundred home health care agencies. The record of compliance by those regulated is commendable. The filled-out questionnaires accumulate in massive stacks in Sacramento. These are stored alongside hundreds of thousands of submittals from citizens under the purview of the agency. The cost to fill out the more than fifty forms required is estimated at $6 million a year. Some critics who have questioned this particular bureaucratic process in California charge that none of the data are used by the agency. Be that as it may, the presence of the regulator is being felt among the regulated, thus undoubtedly enhancing conformance with the law, whether the data are massaged or not. Admittedly the questionnaires which this agency sends out may ask some of the same questions that have been asked before, but this is only because there are numerous units in the agency with interest in the same data. A citizen may find himself communicating with several of these units at the same time.

Analysts of bureaucratic inertia have been especially intrigued by the apparent inefficiencies in welfare administration. An estimated 80 percent of the average caseworker's time is absorbed by paper processing and rule-book entanglements. The Federal Paperwork Commission has reported that research in Colorado demonstrated the feasibility of reducing the 2,800 pages of overlapping forms for the 41 federal welfare programs administered by that state to one form consisting of four pages that provide all the information necessary to ascertain federal and state welfare eligibility. The Commission estimated that nationwide adoption of such a form could save at least $6 billion a year.

Lesser Bureaucracies

Large agencies get public attention easily due to the wide impact of their rulings. Others have to work harder to be noticed. The Endangered Species Act of 1973 has enabled the Fish and Wildlife Service (FWS) of the Department of the Interior to make itself better known, even though it is one of the smallest of federal bureaucracies. Using its authority to identify which species are endangered and which are not, the FWS has been successful in stopping or slowing down large projects advocated by other agencies. It defended the nesting rights of thirty-eight sandhill cranes near Pascagoula, Mississippi, when a coast-to-coast highway was aligned in their direction. The project came to a halt when the FWS labeled the alignment as critical habitat for the cranes. In administering its comparatively small budget of about a quarter of a billion dollars annually, this agency must scrutinize the proposed projects of dozens of other federal agencies and examine many thousands of documents each year to control man's intrusion into the animal kingdom.

One interesting federal unit which made a name for itself in a short time was christened as the President's Commission on Productivity and Work Quality (PCPWQ). With expenditures of only a little more than one million dollars a year, the PCPWQ could be regarded as something of a lightweight in the shadow of giant bureaucracies. Yet, from its very beginning, it was noted for the exuberance of its public information releases and its well-publicized efforts to increase worker output. One of its accomplishments still to be remembered was the researching of the weight and water content of tomatoes.

While most agencies grow, some have to struggle just to hold their own. Staying in business is a universal goal that takes much bureaucratic effort. Most people, for example, remember the draft boards of wartime and would assume that the function was abolished when peace arrived. However, even though conscription for military service was ended, the Selective Service System was continued on a standby basis with a budget of about $50 million a year. The program then consisted of registering 18-year-old males and administering clemency for war resisters. With little else to do, the employees of the SSS undoubtedly found time for considerable recordkeeping and planning for the next world conflict. The needs of the System even though it was dormant were not taken lightly. The annual travel accounts for SSS employees amounted to about one million dollars.

Productivity

A recent study conducted by the General Accounting Office indicated that some federal employees produced less than their counterparts in private enterprise. The GAO calculated, for example, that the cost of processing Medicare claims by the Social Security Administration averaged nearly twice as much as the average cost per claim processed at four companies acting for the government in handling similar Medicare claims. This is not a condition exclusive to paper pushers. A study at the Columbia University graduate school of business under a grant from the National Science Foundation disclosed that garbage collection by the average municipal agency costs 69 percent more than collection by the average private company. Of course, such comparisons do not tell the whole story. For one thing, they do not consider the cost of maintaining claims clerks and garbage handlers if they turned their work over to the private sector.

There are sometimes good reasons why government efforts take longer. Bureaucrats themselves are not all happy with the work expected of them. One government contracting officer openly complained recently that 80 percent of his time was spent in furthering social objectives while only 20 percent of his attention was devoted to contracting. He asserted that every government contract was thoroughly burdened with requirements that the contractor pursue all means to accomplish social reform.

Some government assignments are highly specialized or even unique. They therefore cannot be
judged by usual productivity standards. One worker in the Agriculture Department's Marketing Service, for example, devoted the better part of a year
developing a standard for watermelons. He dili-
gently sketched pictures of acceptable melons and
composed descriptions of abnormalities of bad
ones. This civil servant deserved commendation
for sticking to his task even though he was sure
that his standard would get little attention and that
housewives would recognize a good watermelon
when they saw one, without consulting a government guidebook.

Space

The expansion of government activity requires a lot of office space. In 1975 the federal government reportedly had about 500,000 buildings. If
this is true, there should be no question that the
regulators are here to stay. In 1975 there were approximately 130,000 Health, Education and Welfare employees. At that time the agency occupied
nearly sixty buildings in the vicinity of Washington, D.C. alone, and was undoubtedly looking for
more. The Agriculture Department's 80,000 full-
time and 45,000 part-time employees occupy five
buildings in the capital and a reported 16,000 structures in other parts of the U.S.A.

Spending the Money

Maintenance of the far-flung bureaucratic systems in the United States requires stacks and
stacks of budgets, and mountains of money. That
the American citizen pays for plenty of government attention is apparent in the statistics. There

are 80,171 government units in the country, at latest count by the Census Bureau costing each family more than $7,000 annually. Approximately 20 percent of the employed people in the country work for some unit of government.

The budgeted funds go into many funnels. The Government Printing Office, for instance, spends an estimated $400 million per year and perhaps an equal volume of printing is done by other governmental printing facilities. This adds up to a total printing cost of about $800 million a year. In one year the GPO distributed about 100 million documents for the Congress alone.

The Office of Management and Budget has reported that federal agencies produced at least 2,300 movies in a recent fiscal year. The cost of such film work was estimated to exceed $500 million annually, placing the government far out in front as the biggest producer in the U.S.A., if not the world. Comparable expenditures by Twentieth Century-Fox were reportedly $90 million. A unit of the National Archives has tried to compile a central listing of federal film products. The current count is approaching 10,000, which is about one-tenth the number believed to exist. President Carter has focused on this activity in his search for economy.

The federal government ranks as one of the largest advertisers in the country on the basis of an expenditure exceeding $100 million a year for this purpose. This does not count radio and television advertising which the government gets for nothing. The Post Office, for example, while it is not always competitive in other respects, holds up its end in advertising. The estimated total of its spending on ads in 1975 was $13 million. An expenditure of $4 million alone was devoted to instructing citizens on how to have their mail forwarded when they change their address. The Post Office has also used television to promote the greater use of first-class mail.

Under the leadership of officials in a government nerve center, immense quantities of money may be spent to fund long-term studies to cope with some crisis which vocal critics agree will soon destroy the country. After a few years of conferences and trips around the world to study problems at firsthand which might relate to problems back home, a progress report may be issued which will achieve a remarkable blending of the divergent views of a hundred appointed spokesmen. Invariably it will be a treatise of recognized high quality, quite artistically rendered. In announcing its distribution, the information machines will emphasize that this massive assault will yield enormous benefits for mankind. The news will help the populace to remember the crisis, even though it may have passed.

No better demonstration of bureaucracy's productive capacity could be offered than the disgorging of charitable disbursements. The welfare machine is a mechanical cow with an extremely large udder and a million teats. Its esophagus is connected directly to the government coffers, and its anus to the warehouses for used forms and documents. The complex operating manual for this governmental pet is perused thoroughly by the many milkers and sucklings who nourish their dependency at its breast.

The multiplicity of money-dispensing mechanisms in the government offers important benefits to the recipients. The agencies with the purses vie for the favor of those being subsidized. Without an exclusive license, each agency must try harder if it expects the citizens to follow it to dependency.

Many observers will agree that the charity of government is overwhelming. Countless grants are offered for every kind of program imaginable. So much money flows that keeping track of the paperwork is a major operation. Coordination of the hundreds of agencies handling subsidies may contribute to a substantial overhead cost but it is apparently justified by the avalanche of paper needed to satisfy regulations. Just coordinating the coordinators takes a supreme effort. Budgets are so entangled and overlapping that some critics contend that nobody knows who is paying for what. Of course, this is a narrow view. They overlook the fact that all the bills do get paid.

In the United States, a lot of government money is spent on research. Imaginative researchers are encouraged to do their thing while the government pays the bill. Through the National Science Foundation, worthwhile projects are widely solicited and liberally financed. The Smithsonian Institution has also been generous in its support of research into important problems. These two agencies alone have sponsored such impressive studies as observation of the habits of the whistling duck in India, bisexual frogs in Poland, and native ants in Australia. Millions of dollars have been spent on projects such as the communicative capacity of the chimpanzee, mating calls and paratoid gland secretions of the Central American toad, the semen of the Ceylon elephant, and caste systems in the Orient. One outstanding study which has drawn wide interest involves the examination of skulls in Egypt. The people of the United States undoubtedly have benefited immeasurably from such research. However, more than one observer has suggested that a better investment would be the examination of a few skulls in Washington, D.C.

Another recent research program supported by the National Science Foundation was devoted to the environmental determinants of human aggression. This study involved having a researcher stop his automobile at a red light and then delay starting again until fifteen seconds after the light had turned green. The objective was to learn the degree of impatience and aggressiveness of the driver next in line. The limit of patience was signalled by the honking of his horn. Additionally, to measure the effects of various stimulants such as sex and sympathy, the investigators hired a young woman to walk by the motorists. When she was scantily attired, men drivers exhibited admirable patience with being stalled. They were also tolerant when she was bandaged or used a crutch. One senator in criticizing this research suggested that its purpose must have been to demonstrate the potential advantages of organizing thousands of bikini-clad girls and cripples to alleviate emotional tensions at congested urban intersections. Nobody has yet suggested the routing of new highways through nudist colonies to reduce safety hazards.

Fingers have been pointed at the bureaucracy for its alleged lack of effective leadership and its leaning toward the attitudes of Robin Hood and Jesse James regarding sharing the wealth. The social reformers who have invaded the labyrinth are accused of picking the pockets of the hardworking to support those who cannot or will not work. These bureaucrats are accused of taking care of themselves while they spread this benevolence. Examples often cited by critics are the housing and sanitation in New York City. In defense of that great city, however, is the fact that many of its failures were imported from Washington, D.C.

Federal subsidies do have many critics. Sometimes they are people who are not getting their share. Nearly always they are the payers of the bills. They quarrel that a quarter or more of the recipients of welfare money are not legally qualified, and that many are cheating to get food stamps, social security money, and educational aid.

The federal government now hands out about $60 billion a year in direct financial assistance to state and local governments, an increase of twenty times in twenty years. The money flows through more than one thousand separate programs. Since this federal aid constitutes about one-quarter of all expenditures by the lower levels of government, local leaders are continuously under pressure to provide matching moneys so that the federal dole will not slip through their fingers.

A report by the General Accounting Office emphasized the difficulty that state and local representatives have in keeping track of money available from the federal government. Money is cached in many corners of Washington, D.C., waiting for somebody to come and take it. This has created careers for "grantsmen," professional money finders who help the folks back home get their share of the federal subsidy. As of 1976, about twenty states and more than fifty cities had such representatives stationed in Washington.

Some lower levels of government, however, have become skeptical of Washington's generosity. For example, Maryland declined a federal grant of $60,000 to fund a consumer education program when it calculated that the required paperwork would nearly balance the money received. Wyoming passed up more than $300,000 in water-works grants in 1976, lacking enthusiasm for the accompanying red tape.

States and local governments have not always done much better than the federal government in efficient use of money. A job creation program in California, for instance, involved loans to corporations who provided jobs for the unemployed. Of $4.3 million in loans from 1969 through 1974, over $1.5 million was lost through default, representing a loss rate of 36.5 percent as compared with a normal loss rate of about one-quarter of one percent for commercial banks. Of 124 companies participating in the program, 48 defaulted. The California legislative analyst concluded that something should be done about this. In addition to the loss of money, the analyst pointed out that there was a lag of more than a year in reporting on the program, that there were no data available on the number of persons employed under the loan guarantee program in 1974, and that no data were kept on the number of minority, handicapped, and disadvantaged persons employed, although these were the groups that the program was designed to assist. The analyst said that on the basis of available data, which were admittedly meager, it would appear that the job loan guarantee program had negligible effect upon employment in California. Of course, this would not count the benefits to those who spent the $1.5 million.

A California program to obtain payments from responsible relatives of welfare recipients foundered for various reasons. Among them was the fact that about one-half of the computerized billings for the 15,000 relatives who paid were for the wrong amounts. The correction was slow, partly due to an inadequate filing system. About 12,000 responsible relatives who were billed each month did not pay. Nothing was being done about this. Approximately 30,000 forms with names of relatives who might have been obligated to pay something were piled in stacks on the floor of the Business Services Bureau. Roughly 36,000 relatives needed to be asked again to submit information so that determination could be made as to whether or not they were liable for payment. There was a backlog of about 40,000 new recipients who needed to be asked for the names of their relatives who might be legally obligated to support them.

While state and local governments would like to be left alone to wade in their own mistakes, the irresistibility of power and money from the District of Columbia usually sets their course. The federal government has labored mightily to assure that its presence is felt in even the most remote corners of the land. Take Walton, New York, for example. This beautiful and previously secluded village has become well acquainted with the Environmental Protection Agency (EPA) through its new sewerage system which makes the EPA proud, even though Walton still has its skeptics. It all started with the Water Pollution Control Act of 1972, which required that the villages of the United States would enjoy modern processing of their excretions by the end of a five-year period. The planked outhouse which once was a revered symbol of rural America was in effect outlawed by this legislation. While the people of Walton might have preferred to install more septic tanks to replace outhouses, the federal government naturally could not condone each village going its own sanitary way. The problem had to be solved on a federal basis. This entailed the construction of a new sewage treatment plant at a cost of about $6 million, most of which was contributed by the federal government. The law, however, did not provide for the financing of conveyance of excretions from household to plant. This required pipelines costing about $3 million, a bill which had to be paid from the pocketbooks of the townspeople.

Therefore, thanks to the federal government, the town of Walton has now been introduced into the modern world of deficit spending. The town has a substantial debt for the first time. It also enjoys the services of an official county planner who through his expertise can provide guidance in organizing other imaginative community ventures. Some of the citizens of the town reportedly have become obligated to take on additional employment to finance their participation in the modernization. Necessarily some new jobs have been created. Among these are a number of opportunities in the operation and maintenance of the new sewage plant. The federal government has done its part by contributing a federally financed work program for those who need the money to pay their new obligations.

The government's range of interests runs easily from sewage to education. Having secured its control over the public schools, the regulatory bureaucracy has turned its attention to private educational institutions. This intervention has been made possible by the strings attached to federal aid. In 1975 a study by the American Council on Education found that the cost of federal social programs at colleges and universities had increased between ten and twenty times in the previous ten years. It held that federally mandated social programs had contributed substantially to unstable costs at institutions of higher learning. Some administrators had become disturbed by conflicting rules issued by different regulatory agencies and by the mountainous paperwork accumulated in documenting compliance.

Small, private Hillsdale College in Michigan recently resisted what it labeled as the federal takeover of its campus by refusing to accept the federal premise that schools whose students receive federal subsidy thereby themselves become recipients of federal funds by definition. This placed Hillsdale College at odds with the Department of Health, Education, and Welfare, which argued in effect that a dime in the pocket of a student was equivalent to ten cents in the college treasury if the money came from Washington.

Having thus established its presence in most of the country's institutions, the government maintains close surveillance to detect problems that may need attention. Some politicians and bureaucrats in Washington have taken conspicuous delight, for example, in lecturing the city of New York on its flirtations with bankruptcy. That they were able to point out the horrors of deficit spending surprised nobody. Their superior experience in this field is unchallenged. Those who run New York City were quick to respond to such cajoling from the federals. To demonstrate that the criticism was unwarranted, municipal politicians were willing to curtail any activity that did not affect their voting constituencies. Municipal worker unions also offered to do anything reasonable that would not cut employee benefits.

As the level of government regulation of the

American people continues to rise, one note of caution can be sounded. When regulations become confusing and conflicting and too complex to understand, those who administer them may be tempted to use them for personal gain. In the New York City Department of Buildings, for instance, approximately 17 percent of the inspectors were at one time charged with taking bribes. Half the people charged with offenses in this case were, or had been city employees. Analysts of this situation suggested that due to the large financial interests at stake and the array of rules that builders had to hurdle, bribery became a way to get the job done.

Bureaucracy and the Common Citizen

The attitude of the bureaucrat at the public counter may depend on whether his agency's purpose is to give it to you or take it away from you. Contrasting cases in point would be the welfare department and the internal revenue collector. In the first case, the dispenser and the receiver share a mutual interest in seeing the money flow, while in the second case the extractor alone has such interest.

The citizen standing at the counter of the bureau runs some risks unless he behaves in an acceptable manner. What is expected of him will vary from agency to agency. The fact which he must recognize is that bureaucratic rules of conduct exist for both inhabitants and visitors. Instructions must be read, forms must be filled out, and interrogations must be weathered politely. Nothing should be done that will upset the clerks handling the case. With a very minimum of effort they can allow the folder to remain flattened at the bottom of the stack.

Worse than that, even the lowliest bureauling may have enough license to interpret a citizen's rights as his mood dictates. The examiner who grants driving permits, for example, can easily overlook a traffic violation committed during a test if the applicant has tried to be friendly and respectful.

Speaking of driving licenses, the following news item is of interest:

Friday, January 28, 1977

Snared In Snafu
Bureaucratic Battle
By 'Wrong Driver'

BAY CITY, Mich. (AP) — Because James Bailey got ensnared in the clutches of Michigan bureaucracy, his wife has to wake up at 6 a.m. each weekday, dress their two infant children and drive him to work at a crane manufacturing plant.

But Bailey says he won't give up fighting for the free return of his driver's license, which state officials admit was suspended by mistake but now want him to pay $4 to have restored.

His troubles started last September, when someone was arrested for speeding and driving without a license in the nearby Saginaw County town of Merrill. The motorist gave the name "James Bailey" and an address in Carson City, Mich.

Later, when no one appeared in court to answer the charges, the court notified the secretary of state's office, which controls driver licensing in Michigan.

No one seems to know how, but the court concluded that James Bailey of Bay City was James Bailey of Carson City. Notification of the pending license suspension, originally mailed to Carson City, was returned by the post office because no James Bailey lived there.

On Dec. 18, the Saginaw District Court ordered the Michigan secretary of state's office to suspend the Bay City Bailey's license.

Notified that he was being punished for something he hadn't done, Bailey managed to convince the court he hadn't been in Merrill the day of the violation and had never been to Carson City, about 70 miles southwest of his home.

Properly vindicated — he thought — Bailey was handed two "clearance cards" by the court which were supposed to get his license back.

But the Bay City secretary of state's office manager, Dennis Henley, wanted $2 to process each of the cards. He said the cards indicated the violations were resolved, but not cleared from his record.

Jerome Foley, Saginaw district court administrator, advised Bailey to get the situation resolved because the mark on his driving record could make it difficult to obtain insurance. And he said even if he could get coverage, it could be expensive.

A spokesman for the secretary of state said Thursday the Saginaw District Court had been in error.

"Since the Saginaw District Court sent us a court order for his suspension, the only way we can lift it is for the court to order us to lift it," said the spokesman. "The court really took the wrong action by giving him clearance cards. What we need from the court is an order."

While this case in Michigan got wide publicity, the procedural rigidity that it displayed is not rare.

Similar situations are almost taken for granted in some bureaucracies that the public meets often. The personification of the unappreciated rank-and-file bureaucrat is the postal clerk who stand idly at the post office counter at 8:00 a.m. and tells you he can't sell you a stamp until 8:30 a.m. because his time until then is allocated to other duties. At another post office you may find two clerks on the premises, one idle and the other at the counter with a long line waiting. Something keeps them from sharing the work. The reader does not have to be told that these are true happenings. They occur every day. The low image of the post office owes something to the performance of such counter clerks.

Sullen civil servants have not discouraged many people from coming back. Some citizens desire intimate contact with their government, and may appeal directly for special consideration. Any politician or bureaucrat can be excused for having friends and wanting to do them favors. For some politicians such kindnesses may even be the key to survival. A bureaucrat may be better anchored and more resistant to pressures. With few exceptions the deep roots of bureaucracy insure that those seeking special favors will find the government just as unresponsive as other citizens do.

Some of the people under the thumb of the regulator do not give up without a fight. In one illustrative case, a state overseer of dam maintenance tried to persuade the Wallopum Dam District (names changed to protect the guilty) to repair one of its leaky structures. Its board of directors sent him a letter:

> We protest your repair order. We resent your threat
> to empty our reservoir. Keep in mind that we have been

here for many years and we have never had any trouble
—except with officious bureaucrats. We intend to appeal to the Governor.

A few days later the local legislator tele-
phoned to plead the case for the district: "The Wallopum Dam District is trying to resolve the situation. In view of this, I think you should not press
unduly for the repairs. I recently had the privilege
and pleasure of accompanying the governor on a
camping trip to the Wallopum area. The governor
was tremendously impressed with the beauty of the
lake and expressed the hope that nothing would be
done to detract from this paradise. The dam may be
deteriorating but it isn't hazardous. I inspected it
just this week and I am sure that I personally could
produce a urinary trajectory greater than any possible leak in the dam."

To compound the dilemma, another side of the
controversy sent a protesting letter:

> I have been a citizen of Wallopum Valley for fifty
> years and I'll tell you that leak has me worried. We
> have been waiting a long time to get some action by the
> State, as I told the Governor in my last letter. You send
> your men out and nothing happens. This is a big farce.
> Are you trying to protect somebody? We're going to
> hold you responsible when that dam breaks. The whole
> State has so much deadwood that must be cleaned out.
> The government is weak all over the country. You
> could seal the dam with gelatin if you'd use some of the
> Jello in the backbones of the bureaucrats.

Clearly, not everybody is satisfied to wait for
bureaucratic results. Some citizens feel that they
themselves can contribute to governmental affairs
by intruding into the sanctity of the bureau without invitation. They have no idea how disturbing
they can be to the finely adjusted mechanisms in
the labyrinth. They do not appreciate the extensive

training prerequisite to a role in governmental processing. But nothing could dissuade them from their belief that ordinary citizens have an inherent right to participation in government.

Voters who take the liberty of complaining through the chief executive or members of the legislative body do violence to established governmental processes. By communicating via the political sector they may reverse the rotational direction of the bureaucratic gears. To stifle such intrusions, the response from inside may be limited to a polite acknowledgment of the citizen's appeal. If a larger response is unavoidable, the inquirer himself may be investigated to some extent so that he will come away from the encounter with a better orientation.

Any citizen who ventures across the threshold of the bureau will find not one but several civil servants with responsibility for fragments of the problem that he has come to discuss. In its concern for being thorough, the government will not entrust a problem to a single employee. A citizen with a worry will find responsibilities spread both horizontally and vertically, and some may appear to be on the diagonal. This assures a wide sharing of participation in his business. To keep track of their contributions to his dilemma he will probably want to establish a file for the paperwork which is generated. By carefully monitoring the monthly increments to the file he can measure the progress of the government in serving him. For convenience, these records should be divided into subsections and cross-referenced. This will help him in coordinating the activities of his various governmental benefactors.

An impressive file was developed, for ex-

ample, when officials of Northfield, Massachu-
setts, were confronted with the application of a
local farmer for a permit to construct a toolshed
near a brook feeding into a tributary of the Connecticut River. They found that the shed was already built and that the farmer was sheltering his
horse in it. The immediate concern of the local officials was that the horse was polluting the brook in
violation of state and federal environmental protection regulations. According to reliable reports,
the dilemma was solved by adopting the farmer's
offer to pasture his steed at a reasonable distance
while leaving the door of the shed open. He committed himself further to mount a conspicuous sign
on the structure prohibiting entrance by horses.

In the interest of a tidier environment, other
imaginative devices have been tried to keep animal excrement from spoiling the landscape.
Horses have been outfitted in diapers. Dogs have
been provided with roadside rest stops. Cattle feed
yards have been screened from public view. The
droppings of the human animal have also caused
anxieties. Ridiculing the newest sanitation requirements for agricultural workers, there was a
well publicized suggestion in Wyoming that cow-
boys load portable toilets on their horses while
roaming the range, so that the deer and the
antelope could play without being offended. The
government has taken the suggestion under
advisement.

Conscientious regulators are genuinely interested in helping fellow citizens to lead their
lives. The Department of Health, Education, and
Welfare, for instance, has been continuously alert
for discriminatory practices which may damage
the public welfare. One of the outstanding illustra-

tions of this vigilance was the HEW ruling that mother-daughter and father-son banquets which had been traditional at a public school in Arizona could no longer be allowed. When this edict incurred the wrath of the President of the United States himself, wise HEW bureaucrats put the whole idea into suspense. Soon, however, the same regulators discovered that an elementary school in Connecticut had a choir comprised exclusively of young males, an unacceptable example of sex discrimination. Those who would decry such intervention might do better to look to those who legislate rather than those who implement the laws. Somebody needs to define government intentions.

Bureaucracy and Private Enterprise

". . . The Lord's Prayer contains 56 words; Lincoln's Gettysburg Address has 268 words; and the Declaration of Independence includes 1,322 words. But a government regulation on the sale of cabbages requires 26,911 words."—Robert H. Malott, Chairman and President, FMC Corp., Forbes Magazine, March 1, 1977.

There is little doubt that government controls over American industry have mushroomed during the past twenty years. Bureaucrats now have their hands on the throttles of the productive machinery, even though some of them do not know what makes the wheels turn. In fact, in some cases they aren't turning any more. Strict environmental and safety requirements have forced some plant closures. About three hundred and fifty foundries in the country closed between 1972 and 1976 because they could not afford to operate under new EPA and OSHA regulations.

Forms

In recent years the indicated annual increase in the time spent by businessmen in filling out the millions of forms that the federal government demands has been as high as 20 percent. New forms are being added continuously and all of these contribute to the extended time consumed in industrial paperwork. The construction industry, for example, has complained that the FHA takes as much as two years to complete the handling of papers for mortgage insurance on apartment buildings.

The bill for government services is increasing, and the regulators are getting a bigger share of the payment. The cost which companies pay for being regulated is even more impressive. In 1976, for example, it was an estimated $31 million for Goodyear and about $3 billion for General Motors. The total bill paid by businessmen and other citizens, about $130 billion, was enough to provide free food to every American for the whole year.

The effects of regulation run across the whole spectrum of American enterprise. For instance, government statistics reveal that each retail food chain in the United States must submit approximately twenty-two hundred forms annually. This is estimated to require a total of about 36 million man-hours. It does raise a question as to how they find time to stack cans on the shelf or vegetables in the bin.

In one six-month period the Standard Oil Company of Indiana was required to add sixteen more submittals to its long list of regular reports demanded by the government. The computer tape which stored the information that Indiana Standard submitted to the Federal Energy Administration was said to be more than six hundred miles long. One hundred of the company's employees devoted their full time trying to satisfy the federals.

The aircraft industry once offered documentation that the Pentagon paperwork requirement for a large development effort was more than one hundred times as voluminous as for a comparable commercial airline project, about thirty thousand governmental data requirements versus about two hundred and fifty commercial items. The number of pages of specifications was 16,000 as compared with 400.

The small businesses of the country, totaling about 9 million, account for about half the production of the United States. They are most vulnerable to the force of the government regulator. Paperwork alone keeps them struggling. Operators of small businesses claim that they spend 130 million man-hours a year filling out federal forms, not counting tax forms.

A report by the Illinois State Chamber of Commerce says that small and medium-sized companies in that state are required to fill out 165 different forms each year to satisfy the needs of the state and federal governments. The Chamber estimated that this required an average of approximately five hundred employee hours for each business.

Some smaller companies manage to maintain a low profile so that the government will not find them, or at least so that their presence will not be conspicuous to the regulators. Such companies tend to avoid asking the agencies of government for any kind of guidance. Requests for information are too likely to result in probings by government

inspectors. Many companies prefer instead to turn
to hired specialists who make a business of learning the ins and outs of the regulations. Wherever
possible, these firms would prefer not to attempt
translation of governmental edicts for their
employees.

Regulatory Impact

Some regulators tend not to hear the voices of
their critics. They know that they are doing good,
no matter what anybody says. For example, they
have been characteristically reluctant to acknowledge their contribution to the debasement of the
United States currency through inflation. Critics
have charged that inflationary pressures have been
intensified greatly by the avalanche of regulations
poured upon the nation's producers. Among the
most conspicuous governmental contributions to
higher prices was the charge for special mandated
equipment on motor vehicles, reportedly increasing the price by as much as 10 percent.

To deflect criticism, some bureaucrats like to
blame everything on big business. They have found
that many citizens and newspaper reporters will
buy this readily. There is more than a little sentiment in favor of breaking the country's large corporations into small pieces. These bureaucrats
give sustaining support to the Antitrust Division
of the Department of Justice, which has learned
that one of the best ways to stall corporate expansion is to tangle mergers with red tape before they
even get to court. One of Justice's favorite ideas
sympathetically entertained by many official observers was to require companies of large size to
notify the department in advance of any proposed
merger with a smaller company. The marriage of

the two companies then was to be postponed if the department simply expressed its desire to stop it. This would effectively discourage mergers with a minimal effort by the bureaucracy. The simple filing of the department's intention to object could assure years of delay, during which the financial incentives for expansion would be dissipated.

Some government policies tend to conflict. For instance, the United States has a policy supporting exchange of scientific and technical knowledge with other nations, including those behind the Iron Curtain. But trade restrictions have precluded such exchange to the fullest extent. In denying or slowing down the issuance of export licenses for American firms the government obligates potential foreign buyers of American products to develop their own equipment instead. Meanwhile, competitive producers in other lands sell improved products throughout the world with a minimum of restraint. The paperwork for export licensing in the United States has been blamed for six months or more of delay while competitive advantage is lost. While the significance of this may not be easily grasped, the bureaucratic enforcers know what they are doing. They apparently don't see why well-established licensing procedures should be modified for a few businessmen seeking profit from a bunch of foreigners.

Regulatory agencies may grow old but they seldom fade away. Some opponents argue, for instance, that the Interstate Commerce Commission is no longer necessary in view of the strong competition among the various transportation systems. But the railroads have become accustomed to the ICC and perhaps would not know what to do without it. The commission has involved itself deeply in the actual management of the country's railroads. For example, while granting a 10 percent increase in freight rates the ICC required concurrently that the increased income be invested in tracks and equipment. Thus, in telling the railroads where they can and cannot spend their money, the bureaucracy may be denying railway executives the freedom to make the decisions that will keep them in business.

The Union Pacific Railroad waited for more than ten years to hear the decision of the ICC on its application to merge with the Rock Island Railroad. In the meantime the Rock Island approached bankruptcy proceedings and the Union Pacific lost its enthusiasm for the plan. This did not deter the commission from continuing its deliberations.

In exercising its control of the trucking industry, the ICC instructs carriers on what routes they must use, what kinds of loads they can carry, and what prices they can charge. This is in the interest of preventing unfair competition. A manufacturer of building materials in New Jersey reportedly sends three truckloads a week to Tampa, Florida, but is required by the ICC to have its trucks return unloaded on the northbound trip. The company's subsidiary in Florida ships three truckloads a week to eastern Pennsylvania but the subsidiary's trucks also return empty due to ICC rules. While this is a little wasteful of fuel and vehicles, it does give competitors a chance.

Most businessmen would like the government to leave them alone. On the other hand, some are reasonably satisfied with governmental controls. The Air Transport Association, for example, which represents the major airlines in the country, announced that it would oppose deregulation of the industry on the grounds that it would raise fares and reduce service to smaller municipalities. Likewise, the American Trucking Association and the Teamsters Union would argue that less populated areas would suffer if the government stepped aside and left trucking to the truckers.

However, due to federal regulation the price of an airplane ticket from Minneapolis to Chicago in 1976 was nearly twice as much as a ticket between Los Angeles and San Francisco even though the distance is about the same. This is because the Civil Aeronautics Board controls air fares on interstate flights but does not have authority over air travel within a single state. Critics charge that the CAB has dictated so many flights on uneconomic routes that fares must be computed on the basis that only about half the seats on a plane will be occupied.

Some of the regulatory agencies have been accused of meandering from the course originally intended for them. The Federal Trade Commission, for instance, has been desirous of forbidding the advertising of premiums on television. The banning of cereal box premiums, it argued, would assure that the children's hour was not cluttered with spiels about the good things found among the corn flakes, such as whistles, plastic animals, and photographs of sports figures. After restudying its proposed restrictions, the Commission decided to deal with these abuses case-by-case.

While the FTC may be concerned sometimes with problems that appear to be of little importance, it is industrious and certainly does not lack courage. Unafraid of ridicule or failure, it has experienced some of both. There is an uncontested story about a lawyer for the commission who labored long and hard on a case against a large industry and finally threw up his hands in despair because he had not found enough evidence to make the charges stick. His boss, however, encouraged him to persevere since it would be good practice for him. A court later confirmed that the case was without merit.

Any citizen who wants a better understanding of the painstaking efforts of the FTC in furthering its causes should examine the sequence of processes involved in an antitrust case:

1. Filing of complaint.
2. Exploratory investigation.
3. Memorandum to Bureau of Competition asking approval of preliminary inquiry.
4. Review of memorandum by bureau staff.
5. Approval of memorandum by bureau chief.
6. Preliminary investigation.
7. Memorandum asking approval of formal investigation.
8. Review of memorandum by staff.
9. Review of memorandum by evaluation committee.
10. Review of memorandum by Director of Bureau of Competition.
11. Request for subpoena power submitted to FTC commissioners.
12. Commission authorization of use of subpoena power.
13. Motion to block use of subpoena power.
14. Consideration of motion, by a commissioner.
15. Filing of pleadings.
16. Review of documents by Division of Compliance.
17. Review of documents by bureau chief.

18. Review of documents by Division of Economic Evidence.
19. Review of documents by office of a commissioner.
20. Vote by the five FTC commissioners on recommendation to try case.
21. Submittal of case to administrative law judge for trial.
22. Trial.
23. Appeal of judge's decision filed with the commission.
24. Commission's decision.
25. Appeal of Commission's decision filed with U. S. Court of Appeals.
26. Decision by U. S. Court of Appeals.
27. Compliance investigation requested.
28. Review and approval of request, by bureau chief.
29. Commission review of need for subpoena power.
30. Resolution approving use of subpoena power.
31. Compliance investigation.
32. Memorandum requesting court action.
33. Review of memorandum by Division of Compliance.
34. Commission consideration of charges of noncompliance.
35. Suit filed with U. S. District Court.
36. Trial by U. S. District Court.
37. Appeal to U. S. Court of Appeals.
    And so on.

The FTC is not easily discouraged. One of its more ambitious campaigns attempted to force the automobile producers to quit making spare body parts. It pursued this effort even though its own analysts urged that the effort be abandoned. The FTC went ahead, unswerved by estimates that its proposal would raise the price of the manufactured parts several times.

The FTC sprang into action recently to cope with a nationwide shortage of jar lids for household canning. The agency discovered that the General Foods Corporation in the middle of the crisis was using the sales device of packing its freeze-dried Sanka Coffee in canning jars. At the same time it was offering to send its customers a dozen lids in exchange for two Sanka labels plus twenty-five cents. Evidently suspecting something sinister, the FTC wanted to know how the company acquired the canning lids for its campaign. The answer was that General Foods had obtained its supply prior to the crisis and the amount was too small to have had any influence on creation of the shortage. Not satisfied that the answer could be this simple, the FTC moved in on the company, demanding comprehensive reporting on anything that might remotely relate to the company's possession of jars and lids for home canning. Items on the agency's list of required reports included plans for marketing, sales, and advertising, as well as coffee industry analyses and lists of marketing research and advertising agencies involved. General Foods was required to share with the FTC its files of correspondence with such agencies and to provide copies of material related to the promotion of Sanka in canning jars, such as accountings of advertising expenditures, data on sales inducements like discounts and sales coupons, plus catalogs, bulletins, brochures, and direct mailing information. The General Foods Corporation is still in business, largely because it is patient and persevering.

One of the FTC's favorite ideas is to require the largest corporations to segregate sales and profits by product line. By requiring this disclosure of the deepest of corporate secrets and then sharing the information with the companies' competition, the FTC would hope to play its part in running the economy in a more efficient manner. Those skeptics who would question the FTC's motives argue that ideas like this are really intended to assist the agency's antitrust efforts. They say that, by invading the corporate files, its attorneys are better armed to carve up the company.

This plan advanced by the FTC was sanctioned by the General Accounting Office with some reluctance. It had little choice, however, since the FTC and other regulatory bodies have been inclined to give the GAO polite but limited attention when seriously challenged. The FTC's plan was enthusiastically endorsed by accountants throughout the land as they saw the volumes of new work that would be created by the lengthy questionnaires that businesses would have to submit. In digesting the output of the newly employed corporate bookkeepers, the bureaucracy itself would have to expand, thus making work for nearly everybody.

The FTC is not the only agency with imaginative ideas. The Food and Drug Administration, for instance, proposed to require that all oysters and clams be segregated by fishermen and processors so that the point of origin could be traced. Objectors argued that this would increase the price of the shellfish by as much as 40 percent. Confronted with this, and the further contention that the proposed regulation would not accomplish its purpose any-

way, the FDA demonstrated its flexibility by re-
considering its proposal. It still comes up with an
idea now and then.

Some credit must be given to such agencies
that can correct their mistakes quickly—or do anything quickly. In contrast, the Federal Communications Commission reportedly meditated over an
application for a radio station license in California for more than twenty-five years, accumulating
a swollen file of documents and correspondence. In
the most respected of bureaucratic traditions it
wanted to be thorough.

Even though the bureaucracies are loaded with
responsibilities all the way from oysters to sandhill cranes, the legislators keep giving them more
to do. For example, in 1974 the Congress enacted
the Employe Retirement Income Security Act on
the assumption that there was some kind of a national problem with private pension plans. (The records, however, showed that private retirement
systems were generally more strongly based than
governmental plans.) The Congress assumed that
it could spread the risk by having financially
stronger employers help the weaker. This led to
complex requirements whose red tape and high
cost have reportedly led some employers to aban-
don their pension plans. In the first two years of
existence of the law, about 5,500 private pension
plans covering approximately 160,000 employees
were terminated. To assure that the multitudinous
rules to be developed under the act were carefully
drawn, administrative responsibility was assigned to two agencies rather than one. The Department of Labor and the Internal Revenue Service got the job. While the rules were slow in
coming, they followed loyally the tradition of providing plenty of paperwork.

The New Regulators

One trend which has become apparent in recent years has been the entry into government of those who are unfriendly toward private enterprise. Some of these new bureaucrats inherently gravitate toward the regulatory agencies, where the opportunities for the crippling of American industry are plentiful. This new breed of bureaucrats differs sharply from the more traditional agency inhabitant. In contrast with regulators from the old school, the modern social enforcer need not know intimately the business he regulates and may not have much interest in learning. The condition of a given industry itself may have to be secondary to the social priorities.

Once given the initial impetus, the newcomers are hard to stop. The Federal Energy Administration, for instance, quickly established itself on the Washington scene, surviving several attempts to limit its life. Although some observers argued that its accomplishments were confined largely to its multitudinous press releases, the agency continued to expand, placing much of its emphasis on public relations. Its budget for save-energy advertising grew rapidly. Its public relations staff of more than one hundred quickly developed a heavy workload based to a large extent upon responses to its advertising and the speechmaking of its executives.

The enlargement of the FEA was assured by the disgorging of an awesome stream of legislation requiring implementation by the bureaucracy. In addition, to assist the hordes of new employees to make their imprint, the agency itself followed the ingenious practice of prognosticating emergencies and then marshalling its forces to cope with them. In August of 1975, for example, the agency forecasted a shortage of natural gas in the following winter which would severely disrupt the nation's economy. Although this encroached upon the purview of the Federal Power Commission, which was already laying plans for the looming crisis, the FEA swung into action with characteristic vigor. The agency's bureaulings labored for many months even after the winter was gone and the emergency had not arrived.

The new regulators are fearless. When the Arabs scared the trousers off nearly everybody else with their boycott, the FEA did not hesitate to attack the problem. With no background in administering large programs, it launched its system of allocation of petroleum products. Almost overnight it made work for thousands. Its system of price controls stacked in three tiers was an accountant's delight. Starting at the bottom there was the price for old oil, then new oil, and higher than anything was the price for imported oil. The FEA tied the whole system together with "entitlements" which obligated refiners with plenty of old crude oil to share it with those who were stuck with the new or imported varieties. One of the major recipients of this benevolence was a company which was reported to have benefited to the extent of more than a quarter of a billion dollars in just one year. What confused everybody including the FEA was the role of foreign refiners, who could not easily be compelled to comply with Washington's wishes. The regulators were deeply concerned that these foreign untouchables would set the price of oil sold in America at whatever level they chose. Confronted with pressures to remove controls altogether, the bureaucrats weighed one plan which coupled deregulation with a subsidy to importers. This hopefully would allow prices to seek a common level. The plan faltered when nobody could determine where the money for the subsidy would come from. Evidently they forgot momentarily about the easy availability of the government's printing presses.

The FEA displayed an uncanny ability to foresee crises, some of which never happened. To safeguard the nation against a future Arabian oil embargo, the FEA let the Congress know that it desired the power to prohibit the sale of gasoline for automobiles on weekends. Due to numerous protests it was obligated to consider what would happen when vehicles ran out of fuel in the middle of streets and highways.

Trying enthusiastically to catch up with other regulators, one of the first things the National Highway Traffic Safety Administration (NHTSA) did when it came into being in the early 1970s was examine the brakes of trucks and buses. Four or five years later the NHTSA established standards that required installation of a computerized brake system. The cost for each vehicle was estimated to be in excess of $3,000. In the six months following adoption of the standard, twenty accidents were blamed on the sophisticated equipment. Truckers filed a lawsuit and the court granted them temporary relief from the standards. Confusion reigned as the U. S. Supreme Court got involved.

Without even pausing for breath, the NHTSA tried to impose a seat-belt buzzer at a reported cost of $200 per car, and then discovered that nearly half of these warning systems were deactivated as an expression of driver discontent. Not discouraged in the least, the staff of the agency was already working on ways to straighten out this unacceptable public attitude. The NHTSA has tried hard to be of service from the day of its inception.

In contrast, the environmental movement in government mushroomed without effective opposition. The National Environmental Policy Act handbook in a recent edition contained 759 pages. Some critics contend that its very length would dissuade anybody from reading it. But they are wrong. Many ecologists have read it from cover to cover, and then have sounded their battle cries. Their elected representatives have answered the call.

The Environmental Impact Statement (EIS) required by the federal government, or the Environmental Impact Report (EIR) required at state level, calls for extremely thorough examination of the consequences of nearly any project before it can be allowed to proceed. Environmentalists have successfully used this device in a multitude of cases to slow down or completely stop development which they regard as undesirable. Anybody who thinks an EIS or an EIR is not thorough should read a few pages of the volumes that cause sagging file shelves throughout the country. A memorable quote from one of these documents recently submitted: "During the construction phase, use of heavy earthmoving equipment would cause some dust-blanketing of local vegetation. This could be harmful to the teeth of rodents that feed on it."

Environmental legislation has allegedly at least doubled the time required to win approval of a new site for a manufacturing plant. Some projects have been delayed for much longer periods. The inflationary cost of postponement has been staggering. Environmental protection equipment itself has been expensive. The total cost of compliance with federal pollution standards has been estimated to exceed $40 billion a year. This converts to about two hundred dollars per citizen each year, or about one dollar per cough suppressed. While the overall benefits of environmental programs have been enormous, critics and the government itself continue to grope for an economic balance.

The Environmental Protection Agency proposed emissions standards for motorcycles which reportedly would increase the cost of such a vehicle as much as one hundred dollars. According to EPA's own data, motorcycles contributed only 0.15 percent of total hydrocarbon emissions and only 0.17 percent of total carbon monoxide emissions. The evident conclusion was that motorcycles did not constitute a national air pollution problem.

A proposed regulation of the EPA called for a 90 percent decrease in hydrocarbons, carbon monoxide, and nitrogen oxide emissions from trucks. Diesel manufacturers and operators were particularly upset by this. The problem, they said, was that diesel engines emitted only 5 percent as much carbon monoxide as a gasoline engine and only about one-twelfth as much hydrocarbon. Diesel specialists argued that any meaningful reduction below these levels would increase diesel fuel use by hundreds of millions of gallons each year. Some enforcers regard such arguments as self-serving and tend to give them little weight.

Catalytic converters imposed by the EPA were supposed to remove hydrocarbons and carbon monoxide, but were discovered to be poisoning the atmosphere with clouds of sulfuric acid. In recognition of the problem, in 1975 the EPA chose to phase out the devices gradually since the Clean Air

Act of 1970 spoke only of hydrocarbons and carbon monoxide and was silent on sulfuric acid. Those who thought that the agency should wash its hands immediately of the converter pointed to the great expenditures that the petroleum industry had made to convert to unleaded gasoline because leaded fuel is incompatible with catalysts. This required each of the nation's service stations to install additional pumps. Here again, businessmen sometimes tend to worry too much about their money, and too little about the need to cooperate with their government for the public good.

The EPA has tried to broaden itself. It drew up new rules for returnable beverage containers and tried to get the facilities of other federal agencies to comply. The considerable resistance which developed stemmed in no small part from questions about the limits of EPA purview. The environmental regulators evidently felt entitled to require a nickel deposit on all beer and pop containers sold on federal premises. Opponents were fearful that the EPA if unchecked would be encouraged to expand its concept to every department of every supermarket in America.

The EPA, despite its diligence in its crusade for air purity, must cope with its share of criticism. For example, one of the three air monitoring stations in Cumberland, Maryland, was on the top of the city hall. This station indicated that the city averaged nine micrograms per cubic meter of particulate matter more than the federal limit. The other two stations measured about half the allowable limit. The EPA conceded that the higher reading at the single station was due largely to street dust and residential wood burning and not from industrial pollution. However, when asked to support a variance from the standard to enable the more economical operation of a marginally profitable automobile tire plant, the EPA was reluctant.

While the environmental regulators may be intolerant of air pollutors, they appear to be absolutely prejudiced against noise makers. As far back as the people of Canton, Illinois, can remember, the whistle of the International Harvester plant there has sounded the time of day. They liked it, as the EPA discovered when it attempted to have the whistle shut down in the interest of abatement of noise pollution. The mass outcry triggered by the bureaucracy's proposal got the whistle back into operation in a hurry. The citizens of Canton are still smarting from the bureaucratic invasion. They feel that if they want to listen to a little noise they are entitled to it.

The environmental defenders also hate dust, but it depends on who is kicking it up. On a pipeline construction project in a western state, dust control regulations obligated the contractor to station a water tank truck with nozzle to sprinkle the dirt as it was excavated from the trench. While this slowed the job to half-speed, great clouds of dust rose from fast-moving farm equipment on a neighboring property. Agricultural activities were exempt from dust controls.

Planned projects for the generation of electrical energy have suffered delays or have been stopped completely in the interest of a safe environment. Among the numerous examples that can be cited is the Diablo Canyon nuclear power plant in coastal California. The Pacific Gas and Electric Company, in its long efforts to get this plant into operation, had to obtain approvals from thirty-six agencies. Even at that, it was lucky. The plant at least was brought into existence. In contrast, sponsors of the Kaiparowits power project in Utah spent $5 million over a period of thirteen years, mostly for environmental impact paperwork and footwork, and still had to abandon the project in the end. Their surrender allegedly deprived thousands of laborers and craftsmen of employment. Admittedly, though, this must be weighed against the protection of the livelihood and the health of others during the thirteen-year struggle.

One of the most awesome agencies ever put together is the Occupational Safety and Health Administration (OSHA). In the interest of worker safety a well-intentioned Congress created OSHA and populated it with thousands of civil servants. These new bureaucrats poured out a myriad of rules, compliance with which has reportedly cost industry billions of dollars. In the first six years of agency existence, they wrote between four and five thousand regulations which occupied about eight hundred pages in the Code of Federal Regulations. Faced with taking the inspectors armed with this Manual and spreading them among the nation's factories and construction work sites, OSHA could adopt one of two alternatives. The first was to concentrate on those sites where the highest hazards existed. The second was to ask for more employees so that inspection could be conducted uniformly without weighing the degree of hazard. The first alternative would have been discriminatory and was therefore given less favor. (The new administration of President Carter questioned this and took action to set realistic priorities.)

In 1975 OSHA announced its desire to tighten its allowable noise limits. Its proposed lowering of the 90-decibel limit was estimated to cost 13 billion dollars. This encouraged EPA to propose that the limit be set even lower at 85 decibels, which involved an estimated cost of as much as 32 billion dollars. The activities of these agencies also conflicted with those of the Food and Drug Administration. The FDA regulations called for ceramic tile in dairy food processing facilities. But this tended to increase the noise above the specified OSHA and EPA limits. As a result of the differences among the government's watchdogs, milkmen didn't know whether to be sanitary or silent.

OSHA is famous for requiring coat hooks in toilet stalls and for warning farmers that cow manure is slippery. Some of the regulations stir the imaginations of those who comply. For example, one OSHA rule required that fire extinguishers fastened on walls must be placed at "eye level," the exact elevation depending upon the height of the inspector who checked the plant. This standard had far-reaching effects. One company had for many years maintained its extinguishers on boards raised by a chain to a height eight feet above the floor to keep them out of the path of forklift trucks. To conform with OSHA's rule the company lowered them and soon experienced a high incidence of truck-extinguisher collisions. Reflecting on this, the regulators retrospectively saw merit in putting the extinguishers back on the movable boards and weighed the possibility of imposing this on all of American industry.

Another OSHA regulation calls for backup alarms to be installed on vehicles at construction sites. In some cases the agency requires workers to wear ear plugs to protect them against high-frequency noises, which could include the alarms on backing vehicles. A construction worker thus protected must be alert and nimble.

Some of these newer agencies are relatively fast when their appetites are whetted. If tradition prevails, though, they will slow down as their manuals grow and they get entangled with sister institutuions that are more arthritic.

The problem-solving pace set by the bureaucracy is exemplified by governmental weighing of a proposal to move natural gas from the North Slope of Alaska southward through or around Canada. Many agencies stepped forward to help make this decision: the Federal Energy Administration, the State Department, the Environmental Protection Agency, the Domestic Council, the committees of Congress, and the Federal Power Commission. As much as the other regulators try, few of them can come close to matching the FPC record for stretching out decisions. It would think nothing of taking as much as twelve years to grant a license for a power plant. It thus approached the new problem of natural gas transport with experience that was the envy of the newer regulators. This case had an ingredient which assured delay anyway, and that was competition. The El Paso Natural Gas Company was vying with the Alaskan Arctic Gas Pipeline Company for the privilege of moving the much-needed gas. No matter how vital the need, however, paperwork always has to precede earthwork. This is assured by bureaucratic overseers who are unafraid of controversy.

Despite the reputed power of American industry, few companies have been able to deal with this kind of regulation. Probably nobody is better equipped to cope with a bureaucracy than another bureaucracy. A case in point was the intervention by the Council on Wage and Price Stability when the Consumer Product Safety Commission proposed new standards that it would impose upon the manufacturers of power lawn mowers. These safety rules advocated by the CPSC were estimated to increase the price of mowers by about one-third. The CWPS apparently saw this as a potential embarrassment to a government which would like some credit as an inflation fighter.

The CPSC, whose staff perhaps had not been as well schooled in economics, reportedly obligated one company which had mislabeled one of its products to dump all the offending containers. Allegedly no consideration was given to preserving the contents and simply adding a corrected label.

In 1973 the CPSC investigated a plastic ball produced by a Wisconsin firm and labeled it as unsafe. After some time the commission disclosed that it had made a mistake and that the ball was safe after all. In the interim the factory had lost a million dollars and had practically shut down.

Other agencies get involved in safety, sometimes stretching their jurisdiction to the limits. The Department of Labor in 1972, for example, labeled as unsafe a log-cutting machine being operated within California. The department contended that land was being cleared in preparation for the planting of grapes and since the grapes were intended for production of wine to be sold in interstate commerce the machine came under federal jurisdiction. A $600 fine was levied. However, three years later a review commission reversed the department's decision.

The Local Scene

In 1977 a joint committee of the California

legislature held hearings to learn why Dow Chemical Company had abandoned plans for a $500 million plant in the Sacramento River delta. The committee chairman lamented the loss of a thousand construction jobs lasting five years and the loss of a thousand factory jobs lasting a lifetime. He said that it was no wonder that Dow surrendered when faced with obtaining sixty-five permits from nineteen agencies. After two years of effort it had won only four permits. The question was asked: "If Dow, with its size and with all its expertise and resources, cannot crack through the bureaucratic maze and obstacles government has created . . . then how and when can any lesser developer hope to succeed?"

The ponderous bureaucracy operating in California also slowed down companies who wanted to land Alaskan liquefied natural gas on the West Coast. A total of seventeen regulatory agencies was involved, including city councils, county boards of supervisors, air pollution control districts, the State Coastal Zoning Commission, the Federal Power Commission, the Coast Guard, the Environmental Protection Agency, the Corps of Engineers, and the Federal Aviation Administration. Some of the delay stemmed from uncertainty over the jurisdictional boundaries between the FPC and the Coastal Zoning Commission, a new state agency just learning to flex its muscles.

An insight into California-style bureaucracy was provided by a member of the State Energy Resources Conservation and Development Commission during its recent deliberations on the Sun Desert nuclear power plant proposed by the San Diego Gas and Electric Company. The commissioner complained that the file on this one project had already accumulated to sixteen thousand pages in six months of hearings. "We're drowning ourselves in paper," he was quoted. "We may strangle ourselves in our own red tape."

Epilogue

Now after wandering through the maze some visitors may be disquieted. A trip in the land of bureaucracy can be puzzling. But there is no reason to be fearful. Some of the confusion is illusory.

Observation of the bureauling in his native habitat reveals him to be a creature of unvarying discipline, loyal to precedent, and wary of untested ideas. His forte is compliant tidiness—his response to an environment arranged for him, where words speak louder than action. And the voices he hears most clearly are echoes of his own.

This strange world of the bureaucrats is glued together by ancient attitudes and traditions which have withstood the tests of the centuries. Although it may cause some disenchantment among impatient critics, it offers the comforting dependability of a formalized structure built upon a constitutional and statutory foundation. It inherently resists the stimulus of crisis. And that is good.

A tribute to bureaucracy is that so much is expected of it. When all is said and done, everybody—the chief executive, the legislative body, and the people—depends upon it as a last resort. There cannot be any higher approbation. Without the bureau, all would be lost. Neither the hierarchy at the executive house nor the orators in the legislative chambers can match its essential rigidity.

Bureaucracy is complicated and limitless. This guidebook could go on and on. But let us stop here and be thankful that our country survives.

Index